AF848394

ROUTLEDGE LIBRARY EDITIONS: TRANSPORT ECONOMICS

Volume 14

MANAGING A TRANSPORT BUSINESS

MANAGING A TRANSPORT BUSINESS

Business Management in Transport 2

W.S. BARRY

Routledge
Taylor & Francis Group
LONDON AND NEW YORK

First published in 1963 by George Allen & Unwin, Ltd.

This edition first published in 2017
by Routledge
4 Park Square, Milton Park, Abingdon, Oxon OX14 4RN
605 Third Avenue, New York, NY 10017

Routledge is an imprint of the Taylor & Francis Group, an informa business

© 1963 by Taylor & Francis

All rights reserved. No part of this book may be reprinted or reproduced or utilised in any form or by any electronic, mechanical, or other means, now known or hereafter invented, including photocopying and recording, or in any information storage or retrieval system, without permission in writing from the publishers.

Trademark notice: Product or corporate names may be trademarks or registered trademarks, and are used only for identification and explanation without intent to infringe.

British Library Cataloguing in Publication Data
A catalogue record for this book is available from the British Library

ISBN: 978-0-415-78484-9 (Set)
ISBN: 978-1-315-20175-7 (Set) (ebk)
ISBN: 978-0-415-79318-6 (Volume 14) (hbk)
ISBN: 978-1-315-21123-7 (Volume 14) (ebk)

Publisher's Note
The publisher has gone to great lengths to ensure the quality of this reprint but points out that some imperfections in the original copies may be apparent.

Disclaimer
The publisher has made every effort to trace copyright holders and would welcome correspondence from those they have been unable to trace.

MANAGING A TRANSPORT BUSINESS

by W. S. Barry

London
GEORGE ALLEN & UNWIN LTD
RUSKIN HOUSE MUSEUM STREET

FIRST PUBLISHED IN 1963

This book is copyright under the Berne Convention. Apart from any fair dealing for the purposes of private study, research, criticism or review, as permitted under the Copyright Act, 1956, no portion may be reproduced by any process without written permission. Enquiry should be made to the publishers.

© *George Allen & Unwin Ltd, 1963*

PRINTED IN GREAT BRITAIN
in 11 on 12 point Times Roman type
BY UNWIN BROTHERS LIMITED
WOKING AND LONDON

PREFACE

The subject of business management is just as complicated as any of the natural sciences, or law, or medicine, and it calls for a similarly disciplined approach to its study. The mental tools used in this volume, for studying the management of transport undertakings, were fashioned for business generally in a previous volume, entitled *The Fundamentals of Management*.

The subject is approached from the point of view of *the relationships that managers maintain*. These relationships are broadly divided into: (1) external relations, between those inside a business and those outside it; (2) internal relations among those inside a business; and (3) the relation of ideas and aims within the individual manager. *External relations* are divided into those with customers, State, investors, suppliers, general public and competitors. *Internal relations* are examined firstly in the light of the essential relationship that distinguishes a manager. This is his relationship with the organisation that is instrumental to his purpose. Secondly, 'extra-to-authority' industrial relations are dealt with. Thirdly, the relations among general management and the six major management specialisations (finance, purchasing, production, marketing, personnel and research and development) are looked at. The part on the *individual manager* deals with certain integrating and disintegrating factors, brought to bear upon the individual, by the managerial task.

The section on organisation deals with elements under the hands of managers; with elements that make them managers. It deals with operatives, equipment and raw materials. It discusses the problems of division and co-ordination of elements *subordinate to management*. In the chapters on general and special management we are talking about *management itself*, and the way the overall managerial task is divided up. In a sense the two sections reflect the two great divisions in business: (1) the division of 'labour', and (2) the division of the 'headship' of business.

The particular business of transport has been treated very largely from the point of view of the carrier, but almost all the arguments and illustrations are relevant to the problems of terminal and track authorities for sea and air. Illustrations are from all forms of transport, but the reader may feel that references to the British Transport Commission dominate the scene. If so, I beg to be excused on the grounds that the BTC did, in fact, dominate the transport industry in Britain for over a decade. This book was written in the last year of the life of the giant organisation that represented a bold, if not entirely successful, experiment in transport management.

Gerrards Cross W. S. BARRY
December 1962

ACKNOWLEDGEMENTS

The permission of the Controller of H.M. Stationery Office has been obtained to reproduce extracts from the following:

Transport Act, 1962.
Report of the Air Transport Licensing Board, for the period ended March 31, 1962.
British European Airways Corporation, Report and Accounts for the year ended March 31, 1962.
Civil Aviation Act, 1949.
Report from the Select Committee on Nationalised Industries—British Railways—1960.
British Transport Commission, Annual Report and Accounts 1961. Vol. I.
Report from the Select Committee on Nationalised Industries (Report and Accounts)—The Air Corporations.
Report from the Committee on Relations between Employers and Employed, 1916.
Industrial Relations Handbook—Ministry of Labour.
The Financial and Economic Obligations of the Nationalised Industries, 1962.
Report of the Committee of Inquiry into the Major Ports of Great Britain—1962.
Report of the Working Party on the Turn Round of Shipping in United Kingdom Ports, 1948.

Messrs George Allen & Unwin gave permission for extracts from *The Fundamentals of Management* by W. S. Barry, and *Three Dimensioned Darkness* by Captain Lincoln Lee.

The Oxford University Press gave permission for the extract from *International Sea Transport* by Sir Osborne Mance, published by the Oxford University Press under the auspices of the Royal Institute of International Affairs.

British European Airways and British Railways provided the illustrations of their advertising.

The University of London gave permission for the publication of extracts from my own thesis, 'Air Transport in the United States, a study in the economic geography of the growth and function of selected airlines, 1954'.

I should also like to thank Mr F. Clay, of BEA, for his help in reading the draft of this work.

CONTENTS

Part I
The External Relations of Management

CHAPTER I

RELATIONS WITH PASSENGERS, SHIPPERS AND CHARTERERS

There are three main sorts of customers in the transport industry. First there are passengers, and with them their belongings. Very few human beings travel any distance without a bundle of possessions. Secondly, there are shippers, who, as principals or agents, send goods from one place to another, usually to change their ownership. Thirdly, there are charterers who seek to gain by hiring a vehicle. Dealings with these three sorts of customers are sufficiently different to make it worthwhile considering them separately.

It is often said that the industry sells *a service* to its customers. This statement distinguishes the transport industry from those selling goods, and helps to remind us that its products are not tangible. But we will find widespread disagreement on what exactly the service is. To discover the truth we need to look at the customers' wants and not at the industry itself. The array of services can confuse. What is the passenger buying? Is it cleanliness at the terminal, civility at the check-in point, careful loading, a comfortable seat, a hot drink or time-saving?

In fact there are many services involved, but they are not equally important. Some are vital, and others incidental. We have to sort out priorities, so it is not very helpful to lump together all the various services and refer to *a* service.

The essence of demand for transport is that people want themselves and their goods to *arrive* elsewhere. *Arriving* is the main object. A customer may be willing to forgo a particular convenience, but not to forgo arrival at the right destination. Most 'arriving' is wanted at a certain time, or within certain limits of time.

Sometimes passengers take trips primarily for the pleasure of travelling. But these journeys we distinguish by calling them 'pleasure cruises' or 'excursions' or 'tours'. Here arrival is not the main reason for the journey. The journey is an end in itself.

Passengers

Generally passengers' journeys are inconveniences, not things to be enjoyed for their own sake. Passengers tend to regard their position as temporarily worsened. They are not as comfortable, free, or as well-fed as they would have been at home. Their movements are restricted in a vehicle that probably provides few amenities. They have to leave most of their personal belongings behind. They may believe their lives are in some danger. They may spend most of their journey passing through, over, or by, places they have no wish to be in. To them the journey may be regarded as an unwelcome by-product of the process of giving them what they really want—arrival at their chosen destination on time!

The unwelcome by-product from the point of view of passengers is the essential *production process* for the transport company. The only way to give the passengers the *product of arrival* is to go through the *production process of carriage*. It is possible to produce *goods* without getting customers mixed up with processes of production. Production can be in out-of-the-way places, immunised from customer interference. Not so with passenger transport. Passengers are amongst the moving wheels and the to-ing and fro-ing of men, equipment and materials. Management has customers right inside organisation. Organisation that should be purely instrumental to the purpose of securing passengers' arrivals, is complicated by having to entertain reluctant guests.

This is the nub of the problem of management-passenger relations in the transport industry. Both management and passengers have primary intentions that cannot be achieved without engaging in activities that give rise to secondary intentions. Besides trying to be efficient in production processes management must turn thoughts to making journeys as pleasant as possible. And passengers, besides seeking convenient arrivals, seek to obtain incidental satisfactions from their journeys.

The primary intention of securing passengers' arrivals at correct destinations on time, and the secondary intention of making the journeys as acceptable as possible to passengers, are sometimes difficult to reconcile.

Management must make rules and regulations to govern the conduct of passengers. Management must ensure that passengers do not injure themselves or other people, or damage equipment. To enforce rules and regulations management representatives in vehicles must have some authority over passengers, and this is indicated by titles like, captain, guard, conductor, and so on.

These management representatives regard passengers as *similar* units. All appear equal in their needs and in the processes applied to them. The primary intention of the business makes the management representative preoccupied with safety, punctuality, reporting and other operational procedures. But journey-time is also living time; a passenger cannot be kept in a state of suspended animation. So the management representative must take time off occasionally to attend to personal problems that affect only one passenger in contrast to those that affect all passengers equally. Captain, guard or conductor must be prepared to deal with human emergencies that crop up in the process of living through journey-time; remembering, forgetting, becoming sick, thirsty, hungry, and so on.

This need for transport management to combine, with a primary concern for the technical processes of carriage, a secondary concern for the everyday needs and troubles of people, does not make the relations between a manager in a transport company and his passengers similar to those between, say, a bank manager and his customer. Only exceptionally does a manager in transport need to know anything about the individual circumstances of his passengers. Although he must be prepared to deal with human needs he is not very often concerned with individual needs. He is not like the bank manager who has to treat every client as a being apart and as a man who has a problem in some way different from that of any other man.

Managers in transport cannot, in their relations with passengers, take the attitude that passengers clearly get what they pay for. There are good reasons for passengers' doubts. They cannot, like buyers of steel, lay down an exact specification of the product. The secondary intention gets in the way again. Passengers can specify their primary intention but not their secondary intention. They can state precisely where they want to arrive and the time at which they want to arrive, but they cannot be precise about what they expect as minimum conditions *en route*. This provides ample room for doubts.

The manager of a retail store can drop everything, walk out of his office and into the area where dealings are taking place between his subordinates and his customers. Transport management is not so well placed to keep dealings between operatives and customers under constant surveillance, nor has it so much freedom of choice of time for check visits. This is a reason for the development of inspection branches in transport. The inspector's visit is an organisational device, to replace the stroll that the retail manager takes, into his store, to see how things are going.

In the production process of many businesses, external appearances of equipment, and the interior of buildings that house it, are kept to the most economical standard. This standard may well allow for bright, cheerful colours and clean smooth surfaces in the interest of mental and physical hygiene. But the standard is utilitarian. It is not meant to impress. Managers in transport have to modify the usual businesslike attitude because appearances become means of competition for passengers. Organisational elements that should exactly fit the production process must, to some extent, reflect the concern of management for the amount of pleasure that passengers get out of their journeys. Production equipment becomes part of the passenger environment and so must fill a dual role. There is need for window-dressing, and even optical illusions, to allay fears. Production problems must be masked to avoid causing passengers to worry.

And now we must consider the effect of manager-passenger relations on the behaviour of operatives. Sometimes passengers use a manager's name in order to secure some advantage. Operatives should be instructed to ignore such an attempt to deflect them from the normal course of their duties. The cliché that 'the customer is always right' has had unfortunate consequences in other industries, but transport is protected to some extent by standards of safety, and punctuality that must withstand the whims of individual passengers. Any manager who allows, for example, safety regulations to be watered down, on the principle that the customer is always right, cannot tell where it will lead him. On the other hand in transport there is the opposite danger of over-protecting the employee. If it is found that an employee has broken some operational regulation, it is dangerous to shield him from blame. This might well blunt the keen edge of meticulous attention to detail. Because transport operatives work so much without supervision, management must use passengers as a check on operations. The use must be guarded because passengers are to some extent like other sorts of customers in that they are out to get the best of a bargain, and allow the emotion of the 'market place' to colour their judgements. Also if passengers are regarded as a legitimate source of condemnation of employees they must also be regarded as a proper source of commendation.

A difficulty arises because a passenger cannot usually register a complaint as soon as he feels aggrieved. In businesses where the customer can say: 'Fetch me the manager!' complaints can be dealt with swiftly, witnesses examined, and so on, and all in the presence of the employee, who has the opportunity to refute statements and challenge evidence. In transport, by the time the passenger's complaint arrives on the manager's desk, the former may be many miles away, and seldom is it possible to conduct an enquiry in the presence of both passenger and employee. Usually the matter has to be settled by post or telephone, and this is not always satisfactory for the employee. To be scrupulously fair to the employee nothing should be hidden from him. He should be shown original letters—not just copies or extracts. If the employee knows the whole story, he can reply fully to any innuendos that may accompany the main complaint.

If a manager is not recognised he may, when travelling, receive the same service as other passengers. But unfortunately he can seldom, without a conscious effort, see things from the passenger's point of view. He knows the production process, and is likely to be preoccupied with what is right and what is wrong from the point of view of that process, and so add nothing to his knowledge of the passenger's view of the product. What he wants to add to the basic views he already shares with passengers, is knowledge of the marginal niceties that are important in competition.

Managers can demonstrate an attitude of attentiveness to passengers and their problems whenever they are with them. If a manager steps on to the deck or the platform, or into the waiting-room, and appears not to notice passengers because he is concerned with buildings or machinery, his subordinates may not deliberately follow his example; but they may later tend to justify their own preoccupation with process and equipment by the managerial example. A manager should not play-act in his dealings with passengers. If he goes to extremes, and spends too much effort on a single passenger, his example is impossible to follow. He may be considered irresponsible in using a privileged position to allow himself to be unbusinesslike. The manager must convince his subordinates that his interest in passengers is sincere.

Passengers and the general public usually regard transport undertakings as monopolistic. Because a bus is the only form of public transport that runs past Mrs Smith's front door, even though there is a railway station a hundred yards down the road, Mrs Smith is quite likely to argue that the trouble with the bus company is that it has no 'competition'. If Mrs Smith meets with the slightest show of indifference, she will accuse the bus company of a take-it-or-leave-it attitude, that they adopt because they 'know' she has no alternative to using their buses.

There are good reasons for having a special manager to deal with certain aspects of customer relations in transport. But such an appointment is likely to provoke criticism. Passengers are the business of everybody engaged in passenger transport. For one man to call himself Passenger Relations Manager does not seem to make sense, particularly to the sales branch of a transport organisation. Salesmen argue that their job is getting and keeping passengers so what need is there for anyone calling himself a Passenger Relations Manager?

Special passenger-relations managers, however, do a valuable job in handling the special difficulties with passengers, revealed by their complaints. It is advisable to have complaints handled centrally, and with expertise. The geographical spread of terminals, constantly moving equipment, and central planning, make it difficult to trace the origins of mistakes. If the investigation of complaints is left to those who receive them, enquiries will circulate in the organisational network, and cause confusion.

Consumers' Councils have their place in the industry. The vigour of some is encouraged by the fact that it is possible to secure local advantage, at the expense of the whole community. If the price of transport is not closely tied to costs on particular routes, out-of-the-way communities can obtain a substantial subsidy, by getting transport at standard rates. Behind every transport consumers' council are ranged the economic interests of hoteliers, shopkeepers, industrialists and so on.

It does not matter how careful a transport undertaking is, in the treatment of the *person* of passengers, the effort will be of little avail if it damages or loses passengers' *belongings*. Most people take it as a personal slight if something goes wrong in the handling of their belongings. Their feelings are outraged, but the representative of the transport company is never as worried and otherwise upset as the passenger. He cannot be. To him it is a case of a lost or damaged bag. To the customer it may mean an uncomfortable stay in a hotel, living in the clothes he stands up in, or it may mean the loss of something of sentimental value. The transport official's lack of obvious distress can easily be taken as representing complete indifference.

To be sure of good relations with passengers, management must pay attention to that part of organisation devoted to handling passengers' baggage, to prevent accidents occurring rather than to repair damage when it is done.

Shippers

The most common cause of bad relations, between management and shippers, is the failure to understand the point of view of the shipper. When a shipper entrusts goods to a transport company the matter does not begin and end with *carriage*. The essence of the undertaking from the shipper's point of view is the successful *transfer of possession*. This is what he is really aiming at, and carriage is a means to an end. He is not really buying carriage (in the same way that passengers do not buy carriage); he is buying transfer of possession of goods (compared with passengers buying 'arrival'). So documentation is as important as careful handling. Bound up with carriage of goods are shippers' contractual obligations, reputation and prosperity.

Unless management in transport takes this view of the position of shippers, it is unlikely to gear its organisation to their needs. A sign of something being amiss is where the goods, or freight side of the business is regarded as something of a Cinderella, attracting a lower grade of staff.

Charterers

The relationships of shipper and charterer to transport management are different from the passenger-management relationship in one important respect. Usually shippers and charterers regard their dealings with a transport company as being 'in the course of business'. Passenger traffic on the other hand is largely in the course of domestic and pleasure pursuits. Thus the relationship between management and shippers or charterers is generally much more 'businesslike' than the relationship between management and passengers. There is room for the usually friendly commercial relations between management and charterer, but a good contract should be regarded as the soundest basis for their business association.

CHAPTER II

RELATIONS WITH THE STATE

The Railway Age in England began in the 1830's and lasted until the 1860's. It is so-called because during this time a national network was made for the whole island, from a few local lines in coal districts. These were the years of *laissez-faire.* The railways grew up in an age that believed in letting business get on with its job, without interference from the State. The results are pointers to what can happen, if the State does little to restrict competition among transport companies.

Firstly, England was provided with a railway network in an astonishingly few years. Between 1840 and 1855 over 6,000 miles of railways were built. The spirit of intense rivalry 'to get there first' ensured that no time was lost in wordy debate or leisurely construction. The constructors learnt their lessons with remarkable speed and acquired a technical knowledge that became a gift to the rest of the world. The speed and extent of development well provided for the needs of the age. Industry was expanding rapidly and was thirsting for more and better transport. Canal transport was too slow for many new industries and road transport offered no quicker alternative. The motor car had not yet arrived, and there was very little on the horizon to warn of the approach of a vast network of roads, and fast, compact vehicles to use them.

Over some distances the tracks of competing companies ran almost parallel and a comparatively short distance apart. This resulted in some tariff-cutting that benefited the consumer. But in many cases, shortly after a rival disappeared from the scene, fares were raised to an 'economic' or 'realistic' level. On balance the public lost more from land eaten up by duplicate tracks, than passengers gained from cheaper fares.

The general fevered atmosphere of early development became the 'railway mania' of the 'forties. People plunged into speculative deals, and lost money. Some undertakings might have prospered but for fierce, wasteful competition. The luxuriant growth, and resulting over-providing, was checked in a way that was natural in the eyes of those dedicated to the 'dismal science' of Political Economy. The strong devoured the weak, and the strong were left stronger to devour more of the weak. Railway crushed railway: railways swallowed canal and road. Today, when road and air take a share of the available traffic, we have a railway system over-extended and showing signs of insufficient experience of competition in a hard school.

The State was not entirely indifferent to this intensely competitive situation in the early history of the railways. Companies were incorporated by Acts of Parliament, defining their powers and laying down maximum charges. Parliament at the time believed in competition and disliked both private and State monopoly. But from the beginning the State had to compromise. First, Parliament could not accept all applications, and in choosing sought to minimise duplication. By 1840 Parliament began to get worried about the railway companies making private agreements to stop excessive competition. Parliament even entertained the idea of taking over the railways to prevent private enterprise from becoming too monopolistic!

An Act of 1844 delayed action for twenty-one years, at the end of which a Royal Commission reported that it was in favour of, 'leaving the construction and management of railways to the free enterprise of the people, under such conditions as Parliament may think fit to impose for the general welfare of the people'.

In pursuit of these sentiments Parliament continued to permit end-on amalgamations such as Manchester–Birmingham, Birmingham–London, but refused to allow the amalgamation of companies competing on parallel routes! The Railways Act of 1921 was the government's admission that its own experience in running the railways during the 1914–18 War proved that substantial economies could be made by amalgamation and less competition.

There is some similarity between this story and Government vacillation from 1958 to 1962 on the issues of monopoly and competition in air transport.

Should a transport company occupy a privileged position in the eyes of the State, and be protected as a monopoly or near monopoly? No form of transport is ever again likely to be in a similar position to the railways in the middle of the nineteenth century. Private transport is now a stable and formidable competitor to all forms of commercial transport, over comparatively short distances on land. So a near-monopoly position does not mean 'without competition', but 'without other companies competing' in the same field of transport within national boundaries. Even so, should the relationship between the State and the management of a transport business differ from the relationship between the State and any other form of business? Should management in transport be protected from the cut-and-thrust of normal competitive business practices, and the penalties of failing to remain competitive?

A bird's-eye view of the competitive business system shows us a restless community, that progresses by the process of degeneration and regeneration. New businesses are born, grow vigorous and drive their weaker rivals out of existence. On balance the community benefits. Many people gain from the temporary distress of a few. The desirability of competitive situations rests on the premise that gains will outweigh losses.

And this is just the point that one cannot be certain about with the failure of a transport undertaking. If a chocolate manufacturing firm goes out of business, a section of the community may be deprived temporarily of bars of chocolate. If a transport system fails the life of a community may be threatened. People may no longer be able to earn their daily bread, go to hospital, school their children and defend themselves from hostile neighbours. So much in the economic and social life of a community is *derived* from good transport that it is often out of the question to allow it to become bad. On the other hand, all forms of transport cause some public nuisance. Some cause much more than others. Railways eat up land, create noise, shake the foundations of houses, and so on. Lorries are noisy and produce fumes. Aircraft are noisy, and ships may pollute the sea with oil. The benefits of transport are bought at some cost to the amenities of the community. This is more easily suffered if the supply is no more than the community requires. It is only too apparent in competitive situations that some of the nuisance of transport is avoidable.

Capital sunk in transport is often specific to the industry. A lathe, used by a manufacturer of refrigerators who is run out of business, can be used in a hundred other factories. And so it is with a wide range of machine tools used throughout industry. But a vehicle that is not required for transport has little alternative use. Railway tracks or docks that are no longer required are likely to be a complete loss. The failure of a transport system may well represent a severe loss of capital investment for a community.

Finally, transport is a necessary sinew of war, and few countries would be prepared to see a vital transport system destroyed by competition. Not that competition will necessarily destroy, but the State will not run risks, in case its transport should prove inadequate in time of war.

This is the case for a relationship between the management of a transport undertaking and the State, in which the State shelters management by maintaining a near-monopoly. But privilege is not the only ingredient in the relationship. The State also exercises control, to protect passengers and general public. The State believes that in pursuing economic ends transport undertakings are tempted to cut costs and jeopardise good standards. History shows that the State is right in adopting this general attitude.

The powers that the State often takes from management are those of determining tariffs, carrying capacity (volume in vehicle, and frequency of journeys) and minimum standards of equipment and operative performance. There are two main reasons for government control of transport prices. One is that government must be in a position to prevent management from abusing its privileged position. The latter must not be allowed to take advantage of a near-monopoly to charge extortionate fares. Secondly, government has to watch that price wars do not result in cutting costs to a dangerous extent. Carrying capacity is usually regulated to compel adequate service and to control unnecessary nuisance. Standards of performance of equipment and operatives are regulated to minimise hazard to life, limb and property of passengers and general public.

The close relationship between management and State is not altogether good for the former. It can have a stifling effect on normal businesslike attitudes, and can easily sap initiative and energy. Moreover, it can spoil the relationship between the undertaking and passengers and public. Management tends to be suspected of indifference, bred in a position of privilege.

State regulations are designed to prevent changes for the worse in standards of safety. Inevitably they slow up changes for the better. This can become oppressive. Some managers take refuge in maintaining the *status quo*, because it takes too long and is too difficult to make changes. It is very desirable to school transport managers in the workings of the legislature so that they will not be paralysed by restrictive legislation. The close alliance between State and management of large transport undertakings can be irksome in a hundred small ways.

In England the law does not furnish essential transport undertakings with any express protection against industrial strikes. Some protection is needed because many social and political pressures are applied in a stoppage. Most governments are, however, prepared to use troops if a stoppage threatens the life of the community.

If the management of a transport undertaking look to government to preserve a monopoly, is it proper for them to have the normal 'businesslike', profit-making ambitions? Monopoly cannot be preserved in the interests of the few. Whatever advantages flow from State protection must go back to the community at large. But the State's protection of monopoly cannot justify forcing a transport industry to face the cost of unremunerative or not fully remunerative 'social services'. For example, the elements of a transport system that are kept in being, solely against the day the community goes to war, or to avoid a region becoming depopulated, are social services.

If a transport system has to accommodate social services it should be subsidised by government. If the undertaking bears the cost it is, in effect, putting the whole burden of a political decision on to the shoulders of certain travellers.

But when the State gives a subsidy for the element in which it has a political interest, it should not use the subsidy as an excuse for interference in the day-to-day running of all aspects of the undertaking. The controls that go with subsidies are sometimes all pervading. They become the tail that wags the dog. And management rightly resents being shackled in all its business dealings because, for the sake of the community, it has had to take on an unbusiness-like social service.

Happily the day-to-day dealings among government officials and transport managers are often more fruitful than strict interpretation of regulations suggests. In particular, in England, the majority of civil servants are enlightened and co-operative. They see their task as that of bringing together the interests of operator and community. There is no doubt that the very high standards of English transport operation owe much to the advice and encouragement of this small but effective band of government officials.

An aspect of the relationship between the State and management in transport, that is fortunately invoked infrequently, is the legal punishment of transport employees. The industry is peculiar in that careless industrial action often occurs in the midst of the community, and something that might be regarded as of primarily domestic concern in another industry becomes in transport a breach of common law. In this way the law strengthens the arm of management, who by force of circumstances are unable to supervise every vital act of their employees.

CHAPTER III

RELATIONS WITH INVESTORS, SUPPLIERS, GENERAL PUBLIC AND COMPETITORS

Investors

To ensure a good return on investments in transport it is essential to balance the needs of vehicles, tracks and terminals. If money is invested to improve vehicles, it is usually advisable to invest at the same time in tracks and terminals, so that they keep pace with vehicle improvement. For example, there is little purpose in investing in Boeing 707 aircraft, if money is not also spent in building airport runways of the right length and strength. Similarly, it would not be profitable to invest in nuclear-powered shipping without spending a considerable sum of money on port facilities. The ability to balance investment in these three aspects of a transport system depends partly on who controls them. If vehicles, tracks and terminals are controlled by one management then the task is easier.

Railways managements usually control a complete system of vehicles, tracks and terminals within national boundaries. The managements of air, road and water transport undertakings are not usually so fortunately placed. The fate of investment in aircraft, ships and road vehicles lies partly in the hands of those authorities who control airports and airways, seaports and roads. If these authorities fail to do what may reasonably be expected of them, they adversely affect the management-shareholder relationships of the carriers.

The interests of investors are not usually as paramount in transport undertakings as they are in most businesses. The interests of government and the community tend to override those of investors. Managements have less ability in transport to make decisions to benefit investors, particularly where it would be at the expense of other sections of the community.

The area of freedom left, by regulations made in the interests of national economy and public safety, is small. There is little room to manœuvre in the interests of investors.

The management of a transport undertaking is more than usually exposed to ill-informed criticism from investors. While operational and technical standards are too complicated for easy understanding by laymen, this does not prevent them from making judgements on efficiency. This happens because the process of production occurs in front of passengers, and all investors are at some time passengers.

Members of the general public, by and large, do not think and behave towards a nationalised, or local government undertaking in the same way as investors in a private business. If a shareholder in a private business thinks anything about his investment it is in this way. Is his holding in the company worth more or less than it was when he took it over? Is his holding in the company profitable, in the sense that his annual return is, say, 5 or 6 per cent of the value of the holding? The yardsticks are clear, immediate and compelling. Members of the general public cannot readily reckon their personal capital stake in a nationalised undertaking. There is no established market value of the total assets and, anyway, no individual has a right to withdraw his 'portion'. Finally, no member of the public will enjoy profit, or suffer loss, in proportion to his 'share' of the capital.

That everybody in a town or a nation is an 'investor' in a public transport undertaking, is of little practical significance. Everybody's interest is not the same, because they are not affected as shareholders, but as taxpayers or ratepayers. Some people pay little by way of rates or taxes: some pay much. Some are very conscious of the burden of these imposts; others are not. This means that an articulate and critical section of 'investors' may be identified.

When we consider public ownership of transport undertakings, we are not just talking about complete transport systems like the railways. We are talking also of parts of the systems. We may have publicly-owned vehicles running over private track, or privately-owned vehicles using publicly-owned terminals, and so on. Public investment in tracks and terminals is particularly liable to be overlooked.

Ratepayers or taxpayers are not the only group of interested investors. In the case of nationalised undertakings, civil servants, Members of Parliament and Ministers stand as watchdogs for a nation of investors. In the case of a local-authority undertaking, local government officers and councillors represent the interests of a community of investors. This usually means that public-minded people will scrutinise the way a business is managed. These public servants can often extract information that would be denied to a shareholder in a privately-owned company. They are often helped by detailed annual reports, that may be studied further by economists and other interested workers, up and down the country. They may develop into a singularly well-informed group of critics.

This laying bare of management's deeds and misdeeds sometimes has mixed results. On the one hand it keeps management on their toes, but on the other hand may make management over-cautious, for fear of public censure. Again, the mere revealing of the true state of affairs does not mean that politicians are going to be united in praise of success, or united in condemnation of failure. Parliamentary or local government critics of management are likely to be divided. Their assessment of management will usually be coloured by political doctrine, so that the usual businesslike viewpoints of the private shareholder may not be represented. This lack of agreement strengthens the position of management. While the politicans are busy scrapping with each other, they have less time to breathe down the necks of management.

Suppliers

The relationship between managements and suppliers often contains exceptional features. Some vehicle constructors become very dependent on operators. For example, certain shipbuilders and aircraft constructors have geared their production programmes very closely to the needs of a single line-operator. Even some smaller firms, making highly specialised equipment like compasses, depend upon the continued custom of a transport operator. But although suppliers sometimes commit themselves deeply in their relations with the management of operating companies, it does not follow that operating companies will feel tied to these suppliers.

They are prudent in this attitude. There are dangers in allowing a supplier to think nobody will ever be able to challenge his position. On the other hand, if orders are too uncertain, the supplier is compelled to fix his prices on the assumption that each order may be the last. This can be expensive for the operator. Operators may do better by working closely with suppliers of specialised equipment, and by co-operating in long-term planning.

Suppliers of big special equipment are in a particularly difficult position. For example, aircraft manufacturers must rely on very few customers, so that the loss of a single customer is serious. But suppliers of small parts are in a stronger position. Operators need a continual supply of inexpensive small parts, to keep expensive equipment working. Each small part is, in a sense, as important as the whole. Suppliers of small parts will lose much less than the operators if supplies are stopped. Suppliers of, say, vehicles seek to improve their positions by tying operators by contract to buy 'spares' from them. Operators tend to reinforce their dependence upon suppliers of 'spares', by keeping their stocks as low as possible. Managements in all forms of transport plan their production on the assumption that their fuel suppliers will seldom, if ever, let them down. Secondly, the arrangements made between operators and suppliers often provide for co-operation in development. For example, a vehicle manufacturer will often arrange for an operator to do a certain amount of testing and proving, and to share in the cost of development. Finally, we must remember the exceptional position of the 'suppliers' of major parts of a transport system. In road transport the track is supplied by central governments and local authorities. Airports are similarly supplied. Airways and seaports may be supplied by a number of different national authorities. The position of these suppliers is so powerful that it is probably more apt to regard them as partners in providing a transport system rather than suppliers to the vehicle operators.

General Public

It is possible to identify a general public, from the point of view of transport management. They are the people whom transport affects indirectly. Passengers benefit directly from railways when they reach their destinations. Hoteliers and shopkeepers may also benefit from their arrivals. Had there been no ships and no aircraft, Scottish islanders would still be living under very primitive conditions. On the other hand, trains that thunder northwards each night of the week not only benefit passengers; they also cause a nuisance to families whose beds are only a hundred feet or so from passing trains. Humble homes on the edge of airports suffer from the roar of jets at take-off. And in them live people who can rarely enjoy the benefits of air travel, because the price is beyond their pockets. Where many have to suffer for the benefit of a few, managements face exceptional difficulties in relations with general public.

The country's defence needs do little to influence the attitude of general public to transport undertakings. The government may subsidise a transport system in case there is a war, but the general public does not bestow goodwill because of wartime value.

In countries like Britain, press and radio serve a useful purpose in publicising the nature of relations between managements and general public. If feelings run high they find their way into local or national press, and managements are compelled either to mend their ways or explain what they are doing. Sometimes the press does more than indicate what the public thinks about a transport service. It may set out to fashion a public image, that reflects its own views. Sometimes managements of transport undertakings must patiently ride through a campaign of vilification. Not that they should do nothing in the face of distortion of truth; they should redouble efforts to make facts confound words. It rarely pays to answer back. The press has all the advantages when it comes to an exchange of arguments in their own journals. Management are more likely to win the day by solid achievement, on their own grounds of public service.

'*Competitors*'

'Competitors' has been put in inverted commas because sometimes there is very little competition among them. 'Competitors' vary widely in their relationships. Relationships may extend from those of managements of firms involved in only a trace of rivalry, to those of managements of firms involved in open hostility, and a spirit of business in which no quarter is either asked or given.

These variations are sometimes a true indication of the extent to which interests of rival businesses really clash. One business may be in a position of being able to gain only very little at the expense of its rivals. Another business may be able to expand only at the expense of others. A business of this latter sort is essentially predatory. It is characterised by its preying on other businesses. Such a situation is not necessarily wasteful; it may well destroy complacency and inefficiency.

But relationships among competitors are not only influenced by conflict of interests. A number of other factors may affect purely business considerations. One modifying influence is prevailing economic doctrine. At any moment of time in the western world, a number of economic doctrines attract support. But the centre of gravity of these beliefs changes. At the height of the nineteenth century the centre of gravity lay much further towards belief in unrestricted competition than it does in the twentieth century. Advocacy of enlightened self-interest once encouraged businessmen to indulge in cut-throat competition; whereas socialist views on wastefulness of competition, and social distrust of the ethics of enforced bankruptcy, discourage competition. Big corporations are particularly reluctant to create impressions that do not accord with the spirit of the times. Relations among competitors have some connection with public relations.

The spirit of the age may manifest itself in beliefs that are not strictly economic, and yet bear upon the conduct of business. Where social customs restrict display of bad temper in public, favour tolerance and outlaw intolerance, and generally approve a kid-gloved approach to even the sternest of tasks, they may well inhibit the competitive spirit of business.

The association of competitors for expressly limited purposes sometimes produces more extensive collaboration than is intended. There are so many good reasons for managements 'getting together'. Where they want a spokesman for an industry, they may form an industrial or employers' association; for example, the Federation of Master Builders. They may wish to prevent duplication, and to tackle projects that would be beyond any individual firm. For example, the work of industrial research associations has done much to meet the needs of British industry. They may wish to rationalise an industry by regulation of production. Or marketing will be controlled.

Trade associations, conferences, consortiums or pooling agreements are common in the transport industry. They are intended to rationalise services by restricting the freedom of individual carriers. Regulations restricting competition usually include:

(*a*) sharing traffic, among carriers possessing clearly defined 'traffic rights',
(*b*) fixing minimum tariffs,
(*c*) fixing the capacity of individual carriers.

They may go further, and predetermine the share of total revenue on a route for each carrier.

Carriers may also have to co-operate from day to day in such matters as the common use of terminals. They may form an operators' port or station committee. Co-operation may be *exacted* from operators, to help in regulating vehicle movements over common track, for example, by sea and air. Associations may be formed to standardise passenger handling techniques, and to study methods of improving safety. Associations like the International Air Transport Association, and the Shipping Conferences are primarily to regulate marketing. The National Joint Council for Air Transport is an example of an association to represent airline managements in the conduct of the industry's industrial relations.

In the transport industry there are many good reasons for co-operation among its various undertakings, and for restraining excessive competition. But if the competitive spirit is completely absent, something important is lost. There are dangers that the 'fraternisation' indulged in by managers in their conferences and committees may completely destroy the spirit of competition.

CHAPTER IV

ORGANISATION AND EXTERNAL RELATIONS

Is transport basically different from other forms of business? Are passengers, shippers and charterers exceptional customers? Does the organisation for selling to them have to have a character of its own? Does production have to be specially organised because passengers are what they are? What organisation is needed for dealings with the State, investors, suppliers, general public and competitors? Answers to these questions take us to the heart of transport management. This chapter deals with the proposition that, assuming transport is in many ways similar to other forms of business, it does require *particular organisation.*

The significant thing about passengers is that they are not just customers. They do more than just purchase something. Besides being customers, *passengers play a part in the process of production.* They can be regarded as *the raw material* of transport business. Passengers must be involved in an important part of transport business organisation—the part that deals with production. To involve passengers in the production process, at the right place, at the right time, in the right condition, it is necessary to give them accurate and understandable information.

Passengers usually need directions for boarding the right trains, ships or aircraft. They do not have to acquire all of them from transport companies. Some of them are common sense. Some of them can be obtained from maps, gazetteers or other works of reference. But some of them must come from carriers. Hence most carriers have to include within their organisation passenger information services. These services are not contained in a single unit of organisation. Timetable sections, tariffs branches, enquiry points are all examples of passenger information services.

The conduct of passengers at terminals and in vehicles must be controlled to prevent them from doing harm. This calls for more information. The fact that railway passengers have to be warned, by means of a notice in each compartment, of the penalties for the misuse of the communication cord, may not seem on first thought to be a matter of any importance in organisation. But a moment's reflection shows that the organisation for ordering, storing, issuing, fixing and checking must be considerable. It is easy to imagine the organisation required to put ship's passengers through their lifeboat drill.

Information services must also be provided to extricate passengers from a transport system. It is necessary to organise the way passengers leave a vehicle and depart from terminals. It may be calling out the name of a stop on a bus route and warning passengers not to alight before the bus stops. Or it may be announcing procedures to disembark passengers quickly and safely from aircraft. Whatever it is, the pattern of organisation reflects this important need, to furnish information to passengers on disembarkation.

Because there are exceptional risks to life, limb and property, it is necessary to organise for safety. Transport police, security officers and guards are employed to make the carriage of persons and property safer.

As it may be necessary, in cases of emergency, to have someone unquestionably in command, the position of a vehicle commander is extraordinary in business organisation. Not only is he given gold braid, rank badges and other markings, but his authority during his 'period of command' is made unchallengeable, even by superiors in the organisation hierarchy. Thus, the captain of an aircraft may, during flight, give orders that his company president has to obey.

Because passengers are involved in the production process they are able to help themselves to products they have not paid for. Management has to devise means of charging such passengers. Once a passenger boards a bus or train he can help himself to a number of 'arrivals' at different stops or stations, so there must be checks to ensure that he takes no more than he has paid for. Passengers who have paid for a second-class sea passage must be prevented from availing themselves of first-class facilities. An airline must check the luggage of its passengers, to make sure that they are charged for all baggage carried in excess of their free allowance.

People using a transport system must co-operate with organisation to some extent. They must keep their eyes and ears open. They must follow signs, listen for and act in accordance with announcements and so on. The business is organised on the basis that passengers are sensate, intelligent beings, who do not have to be treated like morons. Into this system, built on these assumptions, every so often a passenger injects an insensate piece of baggage. Nothing is more helpless and forlorn than a lost suitcase or umbrella. A constant temptation to the thief, an easy victim to the careless handler, all in all a piece of lost baggage demands a lot of attention.

Because passengers cannot be expected to remain healthy at all times, some provision must be made for prompt medical attention in cases of emergency. As well as falling sick, passengers may injure themselves, and occasionally they may be involved in a disaster. And so transport companies must equip vehicles and terminals with medical equipment and trained staff.

What has been said so far is sufficient to demonstrate that transport undertakings do need special organisations.

The fortunes of most transport businesses are so closely tied to decisions of central governments, both home and overseas, and of local governments, that it is not surprising to find that the heads of undertakings spend a good deal of time on this aspect of external relations. Considerations of status involve the chairmen of companies in more meetings than they would otherwise attend. Companies themselves tend to support the practice of always being represented at the highest level. It is not unusual to find a full-time chairman and full-time managing director, both busy men, doing two jobs based upon external relations and internal relations respectively.

Certain relations with State and local authorities require sections of organisation to deal with them. For example, crew rosters, working life of vehicle parts, schedules of services may all have to be carefully recorded and made available to government inspectors. Inspectors look at such records to find out if companies are complying with their statutory obligations. It may be necessary to have sections of organisation to ensure that a company obtains all the formal approvals it requires.

Rights of way may have to be negotiated with a local authority, or traffic rights may have to be negotiated with a foreign government. Undoubtedly management will have to obtain licences to operate many sorts of equipment, from radios to aircraft and ships. Management will also have to ensure that its employees have obtained all the authorities they need, in the shape of licences. Because vital parts of a transport system are often in the hands of other people, a carrier may have to appoint liaison officers to ensure that the two or three parts of a transport system are reasonably well integrated. This liaison group may, for example, have to feed information continually to a traffic control authority, or alert the proprietors of a terminal to the day-to-day changes in demand, for the facilities they control.

Nationalised or local-authority undertakings have to prepare for the scrutiny by the representatives of their 'investors'. The annual reports and accounts of nationalised transport undertakings are debated in the House of Commons.

In 1958 Parliament ordered that 'a Select Committee be appointed to examine the Reports and Accounts of the Nationalised Industries . . .'. The Committee have power to send for persons, papers and records. The Committee of Enquiry into the management of the Air Corporations took evidence over a period of ten months, and said of this (in reporting to Parliament), 'Throughout the enquiry the Chairmen and senior executives of the Corporations have given the greatest possible measure of co-operation to Your Committee, who wish to express their gratitude to them. This has taken up a great deal of their time, both in giving evidence and in preparing for it, and it has required a lot of effort by subordinates in preparing the necessary papers and charts.'

Relations with suppliers make special demands on organisation. Firstly, in most transport undertakings the job of buying is recognised as an extremely important one. Sections of organisation are set up to deal with buying, under the control of senior managers. These buying sections are preoccupied with problems of delivery to ensure continuity of supplies so that the whole system shall not be brought to a halt.

Managements often have to provide for close technical co-operation between themselves and their suppliers. They may station some of their own employees in suppliers' manufacturing units. In this way they detect errors more quickly, and see that corrections are made without delay. Suppliers benefit from this. They have advice and customers' checks at every stage, safeguarding them from costly mistakes. Sometimes suppliers send their men into the carrier's workshops and offices, to make them find out more about the needs of the carriers. Co-operation among transport undertakings and their suppliers is considerable.

The extensive nature of the 'general public', from the point of view of transport management, is reflected in the organisation of most undertakings. In larger undertakings the Public Relations Manager is important. A lot of time has to be given to journalists. Newspapers have a duty to give publicity to issues that divide the community. They have a duty to expose abuses of privilege and power. The freedom of the press is one of the strongest bulwarks of democracy. But the freedom of the press can be abused: pressmen are not a particular race of men. They make mistakes, and sometimes they are ill-intentioned. Because it is so easy to whip up public feeling about transport systems, it is desirable to have a Press Branch to make some effort to encourage fairness from the press. Transport is a sitting duck. It can never please all the people all the time.

The Public Relations Division of the British Transport Commission was, in 1960, divided into five sections: press, public correspondence, internal relations, radio and television, and features. The Press Section dealt with the news departments of sound radio and television, as well as with newspapers, magazines and technical journals. It also dealt with publicity given to contracts with the Commission. The Public Correspondence Section dealt with letters, telephone calls and personal calls to the Commission's Head Office, from individual members of the public, representatives, such as M.P.s, and bodies such as local authorities, railway societies and so on. This section also fed into various parts of the organisation any useful suggestions they received. It also provided a statistical analysis of public comment on its services during a certain period. The Internal Relations Section had authority to co-ordinate 'the practice and development of management communication throughout the Commission's undertakings'. Its main activities were the briefing of staff called upon to give lectures, or write material for publication.

The Radio and Television Section obtained 'coverage' for the BTC in both sound radio and television. The section also assisted members of staff who had been called upon to take part in radio or television programmes. The Features Section worked on feature articles for journals on particular aspects of BTC organisation. It aimed to present a 'progressive' image by emphasising plans for modernisation.

Publicity was dealt with in a separate division of the Public Relations and Publicity Departments. The Publicity Division was responsible for the writing, illustration, design, production and distribution of all types of publications, posters, folders and miscellaneous publicity printing. It also dealt with Press Advertising and with exhibitions and displays.

Why did the BTC put Public Relations and Publicity in the same department? The terms of reference of the two divisions did not make a clear-cut distinction between the work of each. It was difficult for the BTC to identify a 'general public' that had interests distinguishable from those of customers. It must have been a small minority of the population who did not use the services of the BTC. But with airlines the position is different. Their customers are a minority, and from various points of view their general public is large. This may be the reason why some airlines have a public relations branch reporting directly to the Chairman or Managing Director, and a quite separate advertising branch as part of the marketing department.

Part II

The Internal Relations of Management

SECTION I—ORGANISATION

CHAPTER V

ELEMENTS OF THE ORGANISATION OF A TRANSPORT BUSINESS

The business of transport is no exception to the rule that there are ways of doing business with organisation, and ways of doing business without it. Organisation is something added to, and separable from, business itself. Long before he had even the crudest tools to help him, man carried loads upon his back or head. To this day, all over the world, we find transport businesses without organisation. The rickshaw coolie plying for hire with his own rickshaw: the ferryman running a scheduled service with his own ferryboat: the country carrier doing a daily round in his van: the light aircraft owner who does rescue work in the Alps on a charter basis: all these are examples of the business of transport without organisation.

Transport is organised if the 'head' of the business does the job *with a particular instrument*. In a previous[1] volume, business organisation in general was likened to a piano. 'Each string in a piano can produce a certain musical note, and will not produce any other if the right things are done to it. Each part of a business organisation, be it human or otherwise, possesses certain qualities that organisation needs. Each man or machine is capable of performing a certain task.'

The 'head' of the business intends to create something new by the process of changing what is already there. In order to

[1] *Fundamentals of Management*, p. 56 *et seq.*

begin, sustain and carry out this intention he needs to symbolise what he is going to create, by a plan. In each case his intention can be viewed as something that is independent of his action to carry out his intention. The action may or may not succeed in achieving his intention. The action in each case is carried out through an organisation that is instrumental in his purpose.

At the far end of organisation, there are *objects of change*. In business organisations producing goods these are generally referred to as raw materials. In business organisations producing services they may be customers or clients. In the middle of each organisation we have *agents of change*. These are the immediate and material instruments of change. The blow of a hammer, the cutting of a chisel or the boring of a drill are the crucial acts. In business the agents of change are tools in the widest sense, so that they may be chemical plants, smelting plants, giant presses or garden hoes. They are agents in the sense that they are directed by operatives, who are the third main element in organisation.

When we look at the organisation of a transport business from this point of view the picture is as follows:

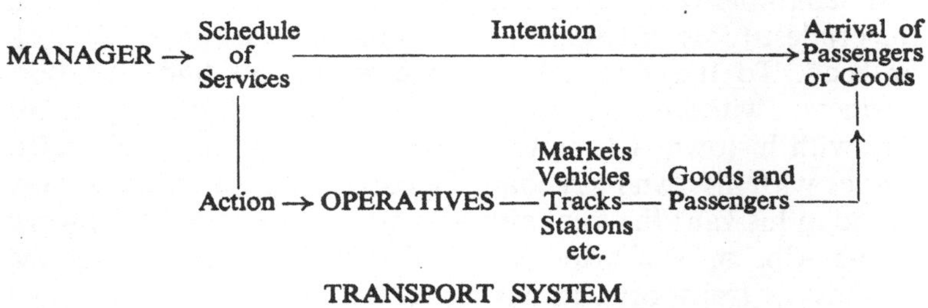

FIG. 1. *A Transport Business Organisation*

This analysis clarifies the position of passengers *vis-à-vis* the organisation of a transport business. They are one of the elements of business organisation. Passengers are *raw materials* just as freight is. They are *objects of change*. In transporting them their positions are changed. They want to arrive elsewhere, but in order to do this, have to become 'raw material' in the transport process of production. Production goes on with the passengers right in it.

The picture we have so far, of the elements of organisation, is from the point of view of the *general management* of a transport undertaking. There may be many special managers contained within the overall organisation, each having his own organisation that is instrumental to his purpose. A manager is distinguished from other sorts of people in business, in that he acts *through an organisation*. Here are a few special managerial organisations analysed in the same way.

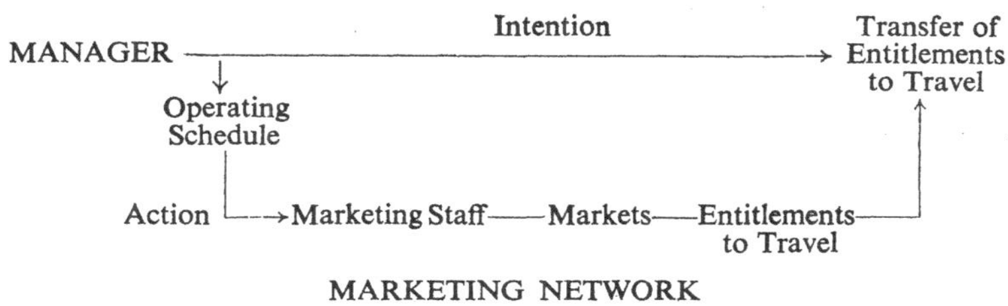

FIG. 2. *A Transport Marketing Organisation*

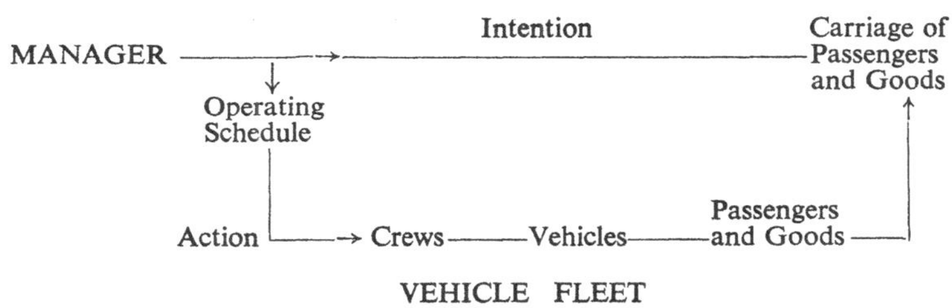

FIG. 3. *A Vehicle Control Organisation*

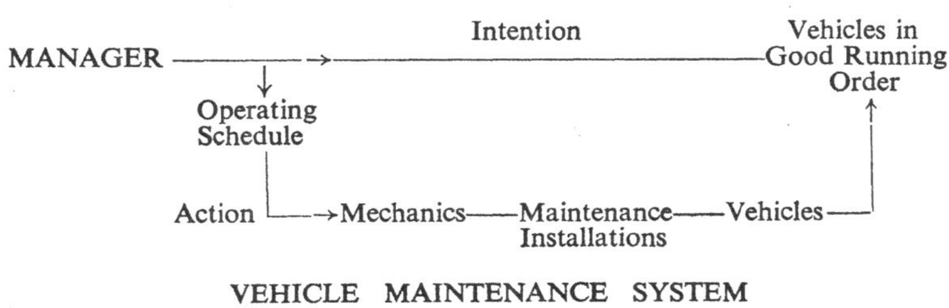

FIG. 4. *A Maintenance Control Organisation*

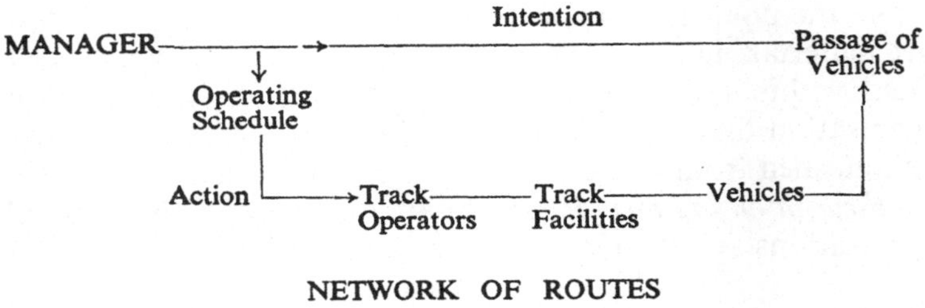

FIG. 5. *A Track Control Organisation*

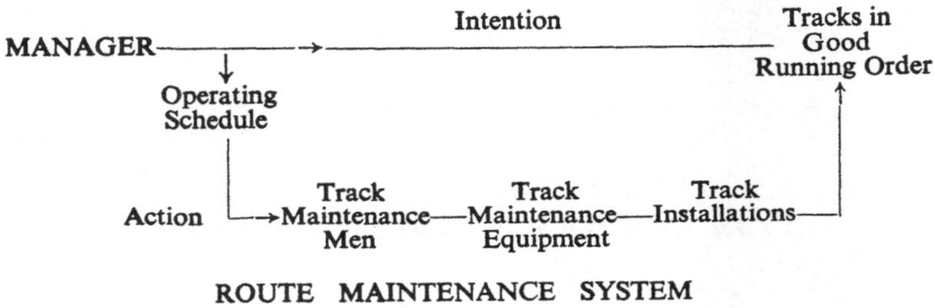

FIG. 6. *A Track-maintenance Organisation*

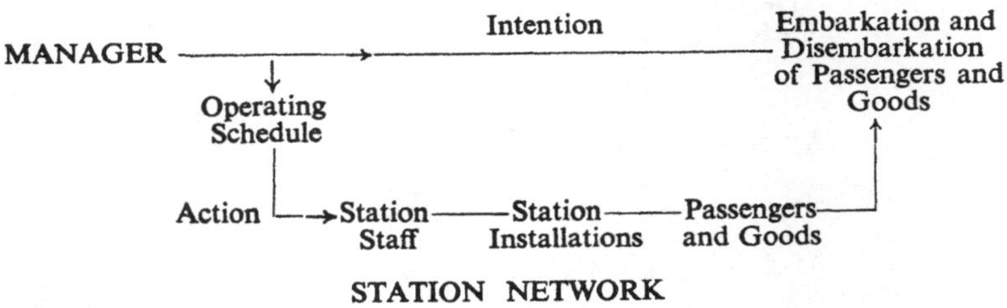

FIG. 7. *A Passenger and Freight Control Organisation*

'Intentions' differ from manager to manager and in the limited field we have looked at, in no case does the 'intention' of a special manager coincide with that of the general management of the business.

The basis of human organisation as we see it at work in business, is that many 'intentions' are built into a single product. Everybody's mind is not cast into exactly the same mould. There is no need to go to extremes with doctrines like 'every part of organisation must have the same objective'. Not every intention can be accommodated; quite obviously a business cannot use a man who intends to rob it. But it can use a man who intends nothing beyond being a good craftsman, and it can use a man whose dominating interest is that of providing for his wife and children. Can anyone short of a managing director have an intention that coincides with the objective of the business? Intention is something we can do something about. The objective of a business is to sell at a profit. The only man who can achieve this is the man who can control both costs and revenue. That is a managing director. Anyone less than the managing director must have a smaller intention.

Successful organisation lies, not in persuading everyone to have the same intention, but in ensuring that every intention *flows from the same plan.* The plan should be the source of all intentions, and it should remain to guide, direct and if necessary compel adherence.

Passengers and freight are not elements in all the organisations illustrated above. Only in the organisations for vehicle control and passenger and freight control do they appear as raw materials. Elsewhere vehicles appear as raw materials. Vehicles are the equipment in one manager's organisation and the raw materials of another's. In one case vehicles are the agents of change, and in the other case they are the objects of change. It is the same with the route network. Differences in the elements of managers' organisations have some bearing on major groupings in an undertaking. For example, organisations with passengers and freight as their raw materials may be put in one division, and organisations with other raw materials may be put in other divisions.

Managers are connected to operatives by expression of ideas. Connection between operatives and equipment is essentially in the exercise of human skill. Connection between equipment and raw materials is essentially that of equipment impressing change upon raw materials. Ideas in transport undertakings are carried by the same media of letters, telephone calls, face to face talks, as in any other business, but also by special media like semaphore signals, radio telephony or radio beam. The administrative skills, accounting skills and social skills needed in transport are not peculiar to the industry. But it does call for some particular skills like driving, navigating, piloting and so on.

The essential difference between transport and other forms of business lies in the change that is made in the course of production. Other forms of business change colour, shape, smell, chemical composition or physical properties. It is the particular job of a transport business *to change the place* of somebody or something.

In setting up a transport organisation someone must first establish an intention of 'arrivals' to be offered for sale. For example, a certain number of seats may be offered for London to Glasgow and return, in each twenty-four hours. The intention may then be made more precise by specifying the way the seats will be spread over the twenty-four hours, say in equal numbers every hour. Secondary intentions may specify first-class travelling conditions. They may involve details like spacing of seats, upholstery, dining conditions and so on. They may also envisage certain regulations such as the limits to the amount of personal baggage a passenger may carry free of charge. They may also be based upon certain assumptions, such as the average speed of vehicles, and the time they have to spend at terminals being loaded and unloaded.

The second step is to take the intention of arrivals, and draw up a plan of operational steps. These should provide a certain number of vehicles, a proportion on service, some in reserve, and some in for maintenance. Account must be taken of cruising speeds and rate of acceleration. The amount of time vehicles stop at stations would be regulated. This operating schedule would then become the guiding light for all branch organisations. It would be established as a permanent reservoir of ideas for the detailed control of the business.

The third step is to assemble men and equipment (markets, vehicles, tracks, terminals, etc.) to deal with the raw materials that the plan provides for. Account must be taken of quality as well as quantity. Men must be skilled enough to use the equipment, and the equipment must be up to date. Operatives and equipment must be properly distributed in place and time. The whole system must be brought into motion by the issue of the necessary instructions.

The organisation can fail for the same reasons as the organisations of other businesses fail. Intention may be wrong. A service that no-one wants may be thought up. An organisation may fail because a good idea is badly expressed in the operating schedule. For example, a service that sets out to provide for commuters may suffer gradual timing changes that in the end make it quite unsuitable for most people who have to be at a desk during normal office hours. Sometimes organisation fails because management has not provided the right operatives and equipment to handle the raw material. Perhaps there is a failure to provide adequate maintenance facilities, so that vehicles are idle for want of essential repairs. Or organisation may fail because management has not given proper instructions to operatives, or it has not given them sufficient training. Men who cannot understand instructions, or who are incapable of handling equipment are sometimes recruited. Sometimes carriers buy the wrong vehicles.

CHAPTER VI

THEORY OF ORGANISATION WITH SPECIAL REFERENCE TO TRANSPORT

Why do some transport businesses have organisation and some of them not? What determines the size of organisation at any particular time? In what order does organisation occur? Finally, what determines the proportions of elements of organisation? Answers to these questions form the basis of a theory of organisation.

There is no simple relationship between size of business, and the origin and growth of organisation. Obviously there is a limit to what any one person can do by himself, so that to expand a business beyond a certain point he would have to employ an organisation. But it may be economic to employ an organisation before reaching the limit of individual endeavour. For example, let us assume that two men sell short river trips, by 25-seater motor launches. The first takes one hour to make a certain trip (including embarkation and disembarkation) and half an hour to sell 25 seats. The other takes three-quarters of an hour to make the same trip, but takes an hour to sell 25 seats. Working separately the result is:

1st man sells and makes 150 seat-trips in a 9-hour day
2nd man sells and makes 125 seat-trips in an $8\frac{3}{4}$-hour day

---

2 men sell and make 275 seat-trips in a $17\frac{3}{4}$-hour day

$$\text{Rate} = \frac{275}{17\frac{3}{4}} \text{ seat-trips per hour} = \text{approximately } 15.$$

If the first man employed the second to drive and did the selling, book-keeping and so on himself, the result would be:

1st man sells 300 seats in a 6-hour day
2nd man makes 300 trips in a 9-hour day

---

2 men sell and make 300 seat-trips in a 15-hour day

$$\text{Rate} = \frac{300}{15} \text{ seat-trips per hour} = 20.$$

In this case an increase in the size of business might *result* from organisation.

The issues involved in a decision to organise or not to organise are illustrated by a country taxi-service, originally run by one man with one car. The owner has to:

(i) borrow money, collect and bank cash, and keep accounts;
(ii) buy and sell cars, buy licences, insurance, fuel, etc.;
(iii) take telephone bookings, keep records of bookings; drive the car and clean it;
(iv) insert advertisements in local newspapers, distribute leaflets and cards drawing attention to his business;
(v) attend to his own personal insurance, national health, pension contributions, etc.;
(vi) try to enlarge his business by obtaining special contracts.

Although the owner talks about a 'one-man business', he does not do everything himself. He has not got *an organisation*, but he does some of his business *by contracting*. Other people help him out in the following ways:

(*a*) An accountant 'audits' his books, and prepares his tax returns.
(*b*) A garage buys replacements for worn-out parts of his car.
(*c*) A garage maintains his car (routine servicings, oil changes, greasing, etc., diagnosing faults, fitting replacements).
(*d*) A friendly rival does the 'jobs' he cannot manage.
(*e*) A manufacturer constructs his vehicles.
(*f*) A builder constructed his garage.
(*g*) Public authorities constructed the roads he uses.
(*h*) His wife takes messages when he is out on a job.

If he wants to expand his business temporarily he can do so by contracting. He can hire cars and drivers from a friendly rival, and make 4d a mile on the deal. He could expand business permanently by creating an organisation, by employing a clerk to do his records, keep his books, answer the telephone, write his letters and so on. He could also employ a full-time driver and spend more of his own time in the office. Eventually he could increase the number of cars in the business, employ drivers, and even bring car maintenance into organisation by setting up his own repair shop and employing a mechanic.

The returns must, however, be sufficient to compensate him for the time and trouble it takes to subordinate elements of organisation. He might consider a fraction of a penny per mile not adequate for having to bother with the problems.

In the end, no matter what personal preferences a businessman has regarding organisation and contracting, he is compelled to behave in an economic fashion. A business organisation will tend to grow to a size that will maximise profit obtained solely by organisation. The process is usually interrupted by decisions to engage in the alternative of contracting. Contracting checks the growth of organisation, but seldom stops it.

Our taxi-driver might decide that £15 a week is the least he is prepared to accept as a return for his own effort. So, whatever way he does business, £15 must figure in the weekly costs of the business.

A conservative estimate, of the custom he will begin with, is 500 'miles-driven' a week. He expresses his operating targets in terms of 'miles-driven'. He can obtain 500 miles-driven a week, in one of two ways. The costs of the two courses are:

By driving his own car	£	s	d	By fully contracting driving	£	s	d
Wages	15	0	0	Wages	15	0	0
Car overheads	6	0	0	Purchase of 500 miles-driven @ 8d a mile	16	13	4
Running expenses: 500 miles-driven @ 4d a mile	8	6	8				
	£29	6	8		£31	13	4

FIG. 8. *Costs of* 500 *miles-driven against a return of* £25 (*assuming a charge of* 1/- *per mile-driven*)

He cannot continue business either way on only 500 miles-driven a week. With a margin of 4d a mile on contracting, he must sell 900 miles a week to just cover wages of £15. To expect 900 miles a week at first is too optimistic, so he decides to aim at 750 miles-driven per week with his own car. He can just achieve this weekly target without employing anyone to help him. But to do even a few more miles he would need help of some sort.

	£	s	d
Wages	15	0	0
Car overheads	6	0	0
Running expenses:			
750 miles-driven @ 4d a mile	12	10	0
	£33	10	0

FIG. 9. *Costs of* 750 *miles-driven against a return of* £37 10s 0d

It then becomes obvious that he could sell another 250 miles-driven if he could produce them. He weighs up the alternatives of (i) obtaining extra miles-driven by taking on a clerk to answer the telephone, write letters and keep records and accounts, to enable him to drive an additional 250 miles a week (1,000 m-d. is considered the new maximum he can do himself), or (ii) obtaining the additional miles from his contractor.

By employing a clerk in organisation

	£	s	d
Wages (self)	15	0	0
,, (clerk)	8	0	0
Car overheads	6	0	0
Running expenses:			
1,000 miles-driven @ 4d a mile	16	13	4
	£45	13	4

By contracting driving in excess of 750 miles a week

	£	s	d
Wages (self)	15	0	0
Car overheads	6	0	0
Purchase of 250 miles-driven at 8d a mile	8	6	8
Running expenses:			
750 miles-driven @ 4d a mile	12	10	0
	£41	16	8

FIG. 10. *Costs of* 1,000 *miles-driven against a return of* £50

At this stage it does not pay him to create an organisation by employing a clerk. It is also clear that a third alternative, of buying another car and employing another driver, would pay even less.

At 1,500 miles-a-week our taxi-owner cannot find time to drive more than 500 miles-a-week if he does office work as well, so he must buy in an extra 1,000 miles-driven per week, or else take on a clerk. He takes another look at the cost of contracting the whole job and compares this with contracting any excess of 500 miles-driven.

By fully contracting the driving

	£	s	d
Wages	15	0	0
Purchase of 1,500 miles-driven @ 8d a mile	50	0	0
	£65	0	0

By contracting driving in excess of 500 miles-driven per week

	£	s	d
Wages	15	0	0
Car overheads	6	0	0
Running expenses: 500 miles-driven @ 4d a mile	8	6	8
Purchase of 1,000 miles-driven @ 8d a mile	33	6	8
	£62	13	4

FIG. 11. *Costs of* 1,500 *miles-driven against a return of* £75

Contracting is profitable at 1,500 miles-driven. 900 miles-driven per week is the 'break-even' point, and there is profit of 4d a mile-driven beyond 900. But his own car 'breaks-even' at 360 miles-driven per week.

By contracting 1,000 miles per week he is relying heavily on the contractor, so he continues to examine alternatives. By employing a clerk he could still drive 1,000 miles a week in his own car, and by buying another car and employing another driver he need do no contracting at all.

By contracting driving in excess of 1,000 miles per week

	£	s	d
Wages (self)	15	0	0
,, (clerk)	8	0	0
Car overheads	6	0	0
Running expenses: 1,000 miles-driven @ 4d a mile	16	13	4
Purchase of 500 miles-driven @ 8d a mile	16	13	4
	£62	6	8

By using 2 cars and 2 drivers—no contracting

	£	s	d
Wages (self)	15	0	0
,, (co-driver)	13	10	0
Cars' overheads	12	0	0
Running expenses: 1,500 miles-driven @ 4d a mile	25	0	0
	£65	10	0

FIG. 12. *Costs of* 1,500 *miles-driven against a return of* £75

At this stage, it would be best to begin organisation with a clerk, so that he can reduce contracting to 500 miles-driven per week. If he could go on buying additional miles-driven at 8d a mile, it would never pay him to get another car and driver. How is this? How is it that providing his own car and driving himself can pay, but employing a second car and driver does not? The answer lies in the taxi-owner's notions about overheads, or unavoidable costs. His approach to his business is naturally that wages are essential for him, so it is necessary to provide for his wages in either organisation or contracting. He does not regard it necessary to add a second driver's wage when calculating the costs of contracting at a later stage. The assumption that he can go on buying additional miles-driven at 8d per mile is a doubt that may eventually decide him to increase his organisation to make sure of the miles-driven he needs.

Airlines often restrict the growth of their organisations, by buying 'hours-flown'. For example, an air corporation shows in its 1960–61 Report an item of 11,523 hours of 'additional flying by hired aircraft and crews'. The careful weighing of alternatives is basically the process employed by the management of any transport undertaking when it comes to ask itself the question, whether or not to increase its organisation. Contracting may temporarily check the growth of organisation to the size where it maximises profits solely from organisation.

The next question we have to consider is what is the order in which organisation occurs? What decides what tasks shall be subordinated to the head of the business?

In general it pays a man in our taxi-owner's position to subordinate that task in which he has greater (or greatest) disadvantage, or less (or least) advantage. Advantage may be in skill, but also in something accidental from a personal point of view. For example, considerable unemployment among clerks, mechanics or drivers, may reduce the value of their skills. The value of skills *from the point of view of the business*, may be expressed as an inverse ratio of the cost of providing them. Thus, if the taxi-owner could do no better than an employee at the job of clerking, the value of his clerking skill to the business would be less, if he required to be paid more for it.

The taxi-owner expects to draw £15 per week whether he does clerical work or drives. He can employ a clerk for £8 a week and a driver for £13 10s 0d a week, for doing work he would otherwise do. He is at the greater disadvantage in clerical work, in that he can buy this skill at a saving of £7 a week, as against a saving of £1 10s 0d a week in employing a driver. Savings of this order can, of course, be fully achieved only if there is a week's work for both.

In practice, managements of large transport undertakings can seldom entertain the idea of reverting to completely contracting. Even the taxi-owner would have had to consider very carefully the possible capital loss in selling his car. The break-up

	Clerking—Skill content x	Driving—Skill content y
Taxi-owner	$\frac{x}{15}$	$\frac{y}{15}$
An employee	$\frac{x}{8}$	$\frac{2y}{27}$

FIG. 13. *Showing relative values to the business of taxi-owner's and employee's skills in clerking and driving*

value of large undertakings may be much smaller than their value as going concerns. This is only one side of the picture. Another side concerns the human element in organisation. Wholesale redundancy alarms both public and trade unions, and is considered only as a last resort. Business organisations are easier to build than to dismember. They have inbuilt tendencies to survive. It is very difficult to cut back organisation when business begins to shrink.

Professor Parkinson makes great play with the tendency for organisation to grow as business dwindles. His amusing treatment of the subject may, however, mislead us into thinking that there is never a good reason for it. If we make the initial mental distinction between business and organisation, and accept the theory of organisation outlined here, we can see that it is quite possible for organisation to grow as business shrinks, *if a change is made from contracting to organisation.* As soon as business begins to decline, the head of a business may decide to do as much as possible within his own organisation in order to keep it intact, and in his efforts to stop all contracting he makes it necessary to increase the size of his organisation. Because of the widespread misconception springing from the so-called Parkinson's Law we must emphasise that there are circumstances in which a growth in organisation quite properly follows a decline in business. Those circumstances are where work under contract is cut down in the interests of keeping an organisation intact.

In 1962 the British Transport Commission announced that about 20,000 railwaymen in the main railway workshops were expected to lose their jobs. The Unions urged the Commission to review railway work contracted to private companies, instead of being carried out within the workshops organisation. The Unions argued that because an Act of Parliament prevented the railway workshops from taking on outside work, there was an obligation to see that they did what was properly theirs. The Commission pointed out the restrictions that management meets in practice, when it comes to consider the alternatives of organising and contracting. Much of the contracting work done for the railways was covered by patents held by the contractors. Contractors' organisations are protected by these patents, and it might be argued that the unions were seeking to keep nationalised railway organisation intact at the expense of the organisation of private companies.

The extent to which British Railways contracted during the years 1958–61 is indicated by the following table:

	Contractors £million	Railways Workshops £million
Locomotives	108	33
Wagons	9	47
Coaches and multiple units	45	48
Power equipment	52	—
Other equipment	16	1
Total	230	129

FIG. 14. *British Railways—Locomotives, rolling stock and other capital equipment—value of orders for* 1958, 1959, 1960 *and* 1961

This table suggests that there is considerable work that could be removed from contractors into railway workshops. At the same time it reveals a high degree of existing railway organisation. How many businesses contain, within their organisation, provisions for the manufacture, or construction, of their own capital equipment?

The third major question we have to look at, to establish a theory of transport organisation, is what determines the proportions of the physical elements they contain? The only practicable way of *measuring* these elements is by the money that is spent on each during the accounting period.

	£000,000
Expenditure on organisation	
Management (administrative charges)	43
Operatives' wages	264
Use of *capital equipment*	
depreciation of vehicles, depots, compensation, renewals, insurance	56
Buying of *consumable equipment*	
fuel, tyres, lubricants, sheets, ropes, etc.	77
Buying of raw materials—publicity	2
Expenditure on contracting	
Line and maintenance equipment, processing of raw materials	48
	490
Miscellaneous	50
	540

FIG. 15. *British Road Services—Annual Expenditure during typical years in late* 1950'*s and early* 1960'*s*

If we convert these figures into percentages of total expenditure we get the following picture:

Management	Operatives' Wages	Use of Equipment	Buying Raw Materials	Contracting
8%	48·8%	24·6%	0·4%	8·8%

A broadly comparable analysis of the expenditure of a large airline in 1961–62 is as follows:

Management	Operatives' Wages	Use of Equipment	Buying Raw Materials	Contracting
5·2%	31·3%	38·2%	1·5%	15·2%

This evaluation does not establish *permanent proportions* of elements. It is an approximate measure of the cost of *bringing elements into use* in organisation. Quantities of equipment and raw materials and numbers of operatives do not have much significance, because they take no account of quality or of usage, and cannot be reduced to a single standard for comparative purposes. So we cannot go beyond asking what determines the *proportions of the costs of bringing elements into use* in organisation?

The extent of organisation determines the proportions of the costs of bringing elements into use. The more highly organised a business is, the higher are operatives' wages and equipment costs, in relation to cost of raw materials. Contracting can influence these proportions in two ways. Contracting may reduce costs of bringing operatives and equipment into use, and secondly may increase the cost of bringing raw materials into use.

These proportions in passenger transport undertakings generally reflect the fact that passengers are relatively 'unfinished' sorts of raw materials. A furniture dealer's raw materials might vary in state from rough-sawn timber to completely finished chairs and tables. If he buys rough-sawn timber and manufactures furniture in his own workshops, then raw material costs will be low, relative to the cost of labour and equipment. If he buys ready-made furniture, raw material costs will be high, in relation to labour and equipment costs.

The cost of buying passengers, the raw materials of transport, may include such items as commission paid to travel agents, advertising, information, materials, accommodation charges and so on. But the degree of finish that can be given to passengers *from the point of view of a carrier* is relatively small. They can be brought to terminals and then conducted to vehicles by agents. Coach passengers can be sustained during their journeys by contractual arrangements for feeding. An airline may incur additional raw material costs by paying a passenger's hotel bill for an overnight stop, or a shipping company may incur additional raw material costs in providing the services of a ship's doctor.

	£00,000
Management (administration)	5
Operatives' wages	84
Use of equipment: Operating	21
Maintenance	12
Buying of raw materials—publicity	1
Contracting—hire of equipment and crews	27
	150

FIG. 16. *Annual costs of a shipping company*

These expressed as percentages are:

Management	Operatives' Wages	Use of Equipment	Buying Raw Materials	Contracting
3·3%	56%	22%	0·6%	18%

Major contracting by managements of transport undertakings may be summarised as follows:

(i) manufacture of capital equipment (buildings, terminals, depots, workshops, etc., vehicles, tracks, communications, machine tools, etc.);
(ii) maintenance of equipment (repairs and overhauls of vehicles and track);
(iii) temporary additions to equipment (hire of vehicles);
(iv) temporary additions to operating strength (chartering vehicles and crews);
(v) processing raw materials (carriage by other operators, other operators conducting formalities at stations, ports, etc.);
(vi) buying raw materials through agents (travel agents—a special feature of the industry).

The proportions of the costs of bringing elements into use in transport business organisations result from the nature of the industry expressed in managerial decisions on contracting.

CHAPTER VII

COSTS AND SAVINGS OF ORGANISATION

Railways in Britain developed a tradition of self-sufficiency during the first few decades of existence. Very soon after the central repair shops were set up in Crewe, they were making equipment for a railway, ranging from power plants and tracks to artificial limbs for disabled operatives. On one occasion a business obtained a legal injunction to prevent the London and North Western Railways from setting up as a contractor for the supply of equipment to other railways. In 1962 railway main shops employed some 56,000 operatives, and a further 55,000 were employed in smaller establishments.

The Transport Act of 1962, which reorganised the nationalised transport undertakings set up by the Transport Act 1947, restricted management's power to bring certain activities into organisation. Powers of manufacture and production of the four newly-created Boards were set out, and limited in general terms by Section 13, Subsection (1), of the 1962 Act.

'Each of the Boards shall have power to construct, manufacture, produce, purchase, maintain and repair anything required for the purpose of the business—

(*a*) of that Board,
(*b*) of any other Board, and
(*c*) of a subsidiary of any of the Boards or of a subsidiary of the Holding Company, and subject to section eleven of this Act and to the following provisions of this section, the Boards shall not have power to construct, manufacture, produce, purchase, maintain or repair anything not required for any of these purposes.'

The Minister was authorised, after consultation with a Board, to direct that Board to discontinue any of the activities which they were carrying on in accordance with this section. More specific restrictions were imposed in other subsections of Section 13. For example:

Section 13, s.s. (5) '. . . a Board shall not have power to manufacture, otherwise than for purposes of research or development, road vehicles, bodies or chassis for road vehicles or major components of road vehicles . . .'.

Section 13, s.s. (7) '. . . The Boards shall not have power to engage in the building of ships, except lighters, barges or like vessels of a gross tonnage not exceeding one hundred and seventy-five tons . . .'.

Powers to reduce organisation were given in Section 14 (1) (*e*): '. . . to dispose (whether absolutely or for a term of years) of any part of the undertaking of the Board or any property which in their opinion is not required by them for the purposes of their business . . .'.

Legal restrictions are also found in the Memorandum and Articles of Association of companies privately owned. In particular the Memorandum sets out the 'objects' of the company, which is entitled to organise or contract to an extent that is 'fairly incidental' to the carrying out of these objects. Courts decide what is 'fairly incidental'.

Some managing directors of transport undertakings are inherently reluctant to add to organisation. They treat proposals to increase staff or equipment with extreme caution. Arithmetic has to show a substantial saving before they will consent to an increase in organisation. This habit of checking organisation is very sound. It is easier to add to organisation than to subtract from it. There are powerful political and social forces that make it difficult to dismiss operatives who become redundant. It is also usually difficult to sell off redundant equipment without loss.

Decisions to contract are essentially decisions to do business through other organisations. Without legal limitations, traditions, or personal preferences the inference is that other organisations are cheaper than one's own. How does one organisation work at less cost than another?

Cost, as a basis for managerial decisions to organise or contract, is not the absolute cost, per period of time, of using all the elements of organisation. A firm spending one hundred thousand pounds per annum on organisation must not be assumed to be more 'costly' than one spending fifty thousand pounds per annum. Many businessmen develop the habit of thinking illogically that small organisations are cheaper to employ than large ones.

It is useful to distinguish between avoidable and unavoidable costs. Costs of renewals, repairs to vehicles and tracks, and the cost of fuel, tyres and other 'consumable' equipment are examples of avoidable costs. They can be reduced by less use of equipment. Depreciation on buildings and plant, and fixed interest on capital are unavoidable costs; they do not vary with use of equipment. The distinction is not necessarily the same as that between 'overheads' and 'running costs', or that between 'central charges' and 'working expenses', or that between 'variable' and 'fixed' costs. The distinctions, represented by these terms in traditional accounting procedures, to be practicable have to be arbitrary.

Two new terms have been used here, to avoid any preconceived ideas, that might result from the use of conventional terms. Whether costs are avoidable or not depends on circumstances such as conditions of contract, covering operatives and equipment, the market for redundant capital equipment, and imprecise notions on what can and cannot be done with elements of organisation in the short run. Thus probably all 'unavoidable' costs are avoidable in the long run.

Avoidable costs represent costs of *use of organisation*, whereas unavoidable costs represent the notional costs of having *organisation available for use*.

Decisions to increase business are of two types. First, there are decisions that result in further use being made of elements of organisation that are already available for use. Secondly, there are decisions resulting in addition to existing elements, and so increasing what is available for use. The first sort of decision involves an addition to avoidable costs. The second sort of decision adds to unavoidable costs, and then to avoidable costs as newly available elements are brought into use.

Decisions to increase the use or extent of organisation, are characteristically (*a*) creative, (*b*) marginal, or (*c*) consequential. Creative decisions are those setting up new branches of organisation for new aspects of business. In transport, decisions to create new services to attract new traffic come under this head. Marginal decisions are those making relatively small changes, either by reorganisation or by adding to organisation, for example, to provide for small increases in traffic. Consequential decisions are those that flow logically from creative and marginal decisions. For example, a marginal decision to increase the numbers of vehicles in a fleet might make it economic for a company to do its own vehicle maintenance.

Creative decisions include those concerned with the initial set-up of an organisation. If organisation is to be indulged in at all, it usually has to be a certain size. An air-tour operator may be discouraged from starting up his own airline because it is essential to have more than one aircraft, to provide a reserve in case of technical trouble. A sea-tour operator may be discouraged from buying his own ships because ships must have a certain crew complement, however few passengers they carry. A railway may be reluctant to open a new line because locomotives have to be a certain size, whatever the traffic, and so on. Economists refer to this idea as the indivisibility of equipment. There is a wide range of equipment in transport organisation that cannot be reduced in size, to match small volumes of traffic. So creative decisions are not made until it is expected that new traffic will match the size of indivisible equipment.

Another characteristic of transport is that financial reserves must be heavy. Reserve ships, aircraft and railway locomotives are big and expensive pieces of equipment to be idle. One of the costs of 'maintaining' equipment in transport organisation is a certain amount of duplication of equipment, to ensure regularity of operation. The same principle applies to crew complements. Costs also arise from the need for spares to keep vehicles serviceable *en route*. Ships' propellers may have to be flown from London to Hong Kong, or aircraft engines may be flown under AOG procedures from London to Sydney. Transport organisations cannot be started on a shoe-string. The British Air Transport Licensing Board made the following comment in its 1962 Report.

'As a result of our examination of the financial resources of the independent airline companies we feel bound to put on record the following comments. Though there are important exceptions many of the companies are in our view grossly under-capitalised in relation to the scale of their operations. With even fewer exceptions the funds actually invested in the company are small by normal commercial standard and bear little relationship to the size of the company and its operations or to the need to provide an adequate cushion in the event of the company, as is not uncommon in the aircraft operating business, meeting with operational or commercial difficulties.'

Creative decisions relating to *organisation* must give rise to a volume of *business* sufficient to make an impact on the market. An organisation may fail because its services are too small to get known.

Some marginal decisions add to the use of elements of organisation that are already available. A decision of this sort may be based upon a comparison of avoidable costs (fuel, wear and tear of equipment, etc.) against the costs of contracting. Whether a contractor would have to incur unavoidable as well as avoidable costs will in turn depend upon whether he has elements of organisation already available for use. With marginal decisions avoidable costs (in organisation) can be compared with avoidable costs (in contracting), whereas with creative decisions avoidable costs only (in contracting) cannot be matched by avoidable costs only (in organisation). This phenomenon makes for tendencies to inertia in the creation of organisation, and to momentum in marginal additions to and use of available organisation.

Marginal decisions on organisation have to be watched closely by general managers to exercise control on the growth of organisation. Organisations outgrow the businesses they serve, not always as the result of creative decisions, but as the result of a multitude of marginal decisions, probably made at a fairly low level of authority. Indeed creative inertia constantly encourages the growth of existing organisation by marginal decisions.

Consequential decisions arise in the main from the need to 'maintain' elements brought into organisation by creative and marginal decisions. They are consequences that are sometimes not foreseen. In taking over several hundred men from a port handling agent, managerial staff on the traffic handling side of the shipping company may calculate wages and pensions and cost of uniforms and so on, but not foresee the consequences to other sections, of their decision to absorb several hundred men into the company organisation. For example, they might well omit to take account of the fact that the company's pay section will have to take on a man to deal with the extra work placed upon them. The uniforms section may have to take on an additional person: the personnel section and the medical section may also be in the same position.

National striving for economic self-sufficiency can lead in the end to national bankruptcy. The idea of economic self-sufficiency is incompatible with the idea of promoting trade. Economics primers point out the advantages from trading between one nation and another. Yet national pride causes peoples to ignore these advantages and endure consequent poverty.

Businesses are not unlike nations in this respect. The work, that businesses do for each other, is like trade among nations. By concentrating on the things they are good at, all businesses benefit. Contracting is the business equivalent of trading. Even businesses reduce contracting to a minimum for reasons of national pride. This has happened in air transport, where tiny nations have their own fully-equipped airlines. Such a policy is usually financially disastrous.

British Chamber of Shipping figures revealed that in one month in 1962 there was a rise of nearly 450,000 tons in the amount of idle shipping. Individual tramp-shipowners were trying to make use of their available equipment by cutting rates to attract cargo from other carriers. The tramp freight index fell in July 1962 to its lowest point since the Second World War, with a loss of six points in the voyage charter index to 78·4. The index had fallen nearly 20 points in six months. Yet at the same time Scandinavian shipowners had on order a number of bulk carriers of 20–30,000 tons which they hoped would make it difficult for the British to make a living from their all-purpose, under 10,000 tons deadweight vessels.

The world air transport industry was in a difficult situation in 1962; the only people who could make profits in the industry were travel agents, and tours organisers who obtained cut-price charters, run on 'obsolete' equipment. The dilemma of the airlines is well illustrated by the following extract from the 1961–62 Report and Accounts of British European Airways:

'The reasons for decline in BEA's load factor in 1961–62 fall into two broad groups: those associated with the fact that traffic expansion did not come up to expectations and those associated with the fact that capacity could not quickly be reduced in line with the traffic actually forthcoming.'

BEA had, in fact, budgeted for a 20 per cent increase in traffic, and had experienced only 9·2 per cent. One of the two main reasons for this, given in the report, was competition from the equipment of other airlines. Competitors had introduced jet aircraft on the more important of the Corporation's routes. The Report went on to say:

'In the face of this competitive pressure BEA has endeavoured to increase its own jet capacity as much as possible and seven more Comets were brought into service during the year; Comet operations accounted for 24 per cent of the traffic carried by BEA in 1961–62. Even so there was a decline in BEA's share of the European market. The introduction of more Comet capacity was the first of the two factors which explain *the Corporation's inability to adjust its capacity to the lower level of demand.* Competitive pressures obliged BEA to bring additional jet capacity into service and thus caused some non-jet capacity to become superfluous. A further cause of the inability to maintain load factors by reducing capacity was the substantial increase in the average size of aircraft used by BEA. In 1961–62 the average seating capacity of BEA's aircraft increased to 68 from 56 in the previous year. Even more significant was the fact that the percentage increase in seating capacity was greater than the percentage increase in passenger traffic; average seating capacity increased by 21 per cent whilst passenger miles increased by only 11 per cent. This has happened only once previously in BEA's history—in the difficult year 1958–59—and even then the extent of the divergence in the growth rates was much less than in the past year. When traffic increase is less than the increase in aircraft size it is evident that the average load factor can only be maintained at its previous level by a reduction in frequency of services. Commercial and competitive considerations weighed strongly against reductions in the frequency of service on most of BEA's international routes in 1961–62 and, as a result of this, the total capacity ton-miles operated increased by 18·8 per cent despite the fact that load ton-miles increased by only 9·2 per cent.'

Management was compelled to add to the elements of organisation. The compelling factor was that managements of other airlines were all busy adding to their organisations. Why is it that competition, which seems to be so good for progress in other forms of business, is often disastrous in the business of transport? In most other forms of business it is the product that matters to the customer, who judges respective claims basically on price. Competitive strength is achieved by a business *reducing its costs of organisation* so that it can sell the product more cheaply. But, in transport, competition is largely organisational competition, in the sense that it is the equipment that matters to the passenger, because competitors can all deliver the goods in the shape of his arrival at his chosen destination. So competitive strength of a transport business has to be achieved very often by its *increasing the costs of organisation.*

Some airlines have had political freedom to make managerial decisions from comparative costs of organising and contracting, and have chosen the latter. Cyprus Airways and TAP, the Portuguese airline, ran scheduled services up to 1962 on chartered aircraft and crews. Airline managements sometimes rationalise organisational growth by operating agreements, like those of SAS and Swissair, BEA and Olympic Airways.

A good example of co-operation, to rationalise transport organisations by operating agreements, is that of road transport in the Brighton area. A long tradition began with amalgamation of horse-bus proprietors in 1884. When the Brighton Corporation organised their electric tramway business in 1901 the horse-buses continued to play their part. It was not a decision based on sentiment, but on sound economics, shaped by topography and municipal boundaries. Eventually motor-bus systems developed; Brighton, Hove and District Omnibus Co. Ltd. (a Tilling subsidiary) served *the towns* of Brighton and Hove, while Southdown Motor Services Ltd. served *the country* around and between the two towns. In 1919 Tilling made a seven-year agreement to pay to each of Brighton and Hove

Corporations £40 a year for 50 buses and £20 a year for each additional bus above 50. The bus company agreed to provide services on routes specified by the Corporations, and the latter agreed not to put their own equipment on to these routes, or allow other companies to do so. A number of further pooling agreements were made during the following years: for example, under the Brighton Corporation (Transport) Act 1938, the Corporation provided 20 per cent of the trolley-bus mileage (and had to buy 11 trolley-buses to do it). In 1961 the three undertakings, Brighton Corporation, Brighton, Hove and District Omnibus Co. Ltd., and Southdown Motor Services Ltd., made a fresh agreement. This allowed the Brighton bus company to provide regular contract services in the area, and for Southdown to do the same. Southdown's irregular contract work, such as excursions and tours were not included in the agreement. The parties to the agreement planned to hire equipment to each other, and hoped to hire Corporation vehicles to other municipal bus undertakings, or company vehicles to other nationalised road and railway undertakings.

The successful conduct of a transport business depends so much on managerial decisions to make savings by fully using organisation and to avoid the costs of over-providing organisation, and to contract where necessary, that we must illustrate British Railways' efforts to this end in 1962. In that year they planned to make further use of land they had available as sites for new oil storage and distribution centres, in large towns and cities where land was usually scarce. It was hoped that the oil companies would find it profitable to 'contract' this part of their business to the railways, as the alternative of providing their own land would be more costly. The railways then expected as a consequence that they would run fast bulk trains to connect these centres to refineries and coastal oil terminals. With the country's oil consumption increasing at a rate of about 7 per cent a year the railways believed they were on to a good thing. The interesting question, the answer to which was not known at the time of writing, was would the oil companies agree to contract this vital aspect of their business? And if the arithmetic showed savings by doing what the railways wanted, would they, nevertheless, decide to add to their own assets?

CHAPTER VIII

PRINCIPLES OF SUBORDINATION

A transport undertaking must be highly disciplined. Managerial control of operations must be completely effective. That operatives should be well-disciplined is particularly important in times of emergency. But apart from emergencies, the fabric of the industry is systematic presentation of services. Being regular, frequent and punctual are all part of being well-disciplined. Swift reactions to danger signals are well-drilled responses. The need for discipline extends even to customers.

The industry has signs to mark the need for effective subordination. Uniforms distinguish officials on duty. Badges and rank markings declare their authority. Quasi-military formalities of saluting, and mode of address remind employees of the importance of authority. There are summary disciplinary procedures to deal with infringements of regulations. Behind all this stands the law with courts of enquiry, establishment of guilt, and severe penalties for major offences.

Considerable authority is exercised by employees of comparatively low rank in organisation. Vehicle commanders often exercise during periods of command, authority that extends over organisational superiors. This 'situational' authority is not an exception to the general principles of subordination. Authority that is passed on is not given away. Command authority is a temporary addition to the amount of authority exercised in the organisation, and it is continuously supported by higher sources. A superior subject to command authority is, in fact, subject to his own ordinance or to that of his superior. There are many parallels to this situation. Members of Parliament are subject to the laws they help to make. A company commander will obey a command from one of his own sentries. A police sergeant will obey the traffic signals of one of his own constables.

Breaches of company regulations may lead to disaster involving extensive damage to property and life; employees may incur severe legal penalties for misdemeanour or even negligence. As well as the provisions of common law, there are those of statute law. Merchant Shipping, Air Navigation, Road Traffic, and Railway and Canal Acts strengthen the authority of management. For example, Section II, s.s. (1) of the Civil Aviation Act 1949 provided that:

'. . . where an aircraft is flown in such a manner as to be the cause of unnecessary danger to any person or property on land or water, the pilot or the person in charge of the aircraft, and also the owner thereof unless he proves to the satisfaction of the court that the aircraft was so flown without his actual fault or privity, shall be liable on summary conviction to a fine not exceeding two hundred pounds or to imprisonment for a term not exceeding six months or to both'.

This same Act illustrates delegated legislation that affects the management of the transport industry. Section 8, s.s. (2) allowed provision to be made *by Order in Council* for:

(*a*) the registration of aircraft in the UK,
(*b*) preventing aircraft flying without certificates of airworthiness, and without having complied with laid down conditions of repair and maintenance,
(*c*) the licensing, inspection and regulation of aerodromes and aircraft factories,
(*d*) preventing unlicensed persons doing certain inspection and supervision work at licensed aerodromes,
(*e*) the conditions under which aircraft may fly whether entering, leaving or flying from one part of the UK to another,
(*f*) the conditions under which passengers and goods may be carried by air, and the conditions under which aircraft are used for any other commercial purpose,
(*g*) preventing external hazards to air navigation,
(*h*) generally securing the safety, efficiency and regularity of air navigation and the safety of aircraft and of persons and property both within and outside the aircraft,
(*i*) requiring persons concerned with air navigation to supply meteorological information,
(*j*) regulating communications,
(*k*) the use of the civil air ensign,

(*l*) prohibited areas for flying in the UK,
(*m*) customs controls,
(*n*) licensing certain activities,
(*o*) charges for the use of licensed aerodromes,
(*p*) fees to be paid for necessary licences,
(*q*) making exemptions from various Orders in Council.

The law strengthens the arm of management in certain undertakings by empowering them to make their own bylaws. For example, under Section 67 of the Transport Act, 1962:

'(1) The Railways Board and the London Board may each make bylaws regulating the use and working of, and travel on, their railways, the maintenance of order on their railways and railways premises, including stations, the approaches to stations, and the conduct of all persons, *including their officers and servants*, while on those premises, and in particular bylaws—

(*a*) with respect to tickets issued for entry on their railway premises or travel on their railways and the evasion of payment of fares and other charges,
(*b*) with respect to interference or obstruction of the working of the railways,
(*c*) with respect to the smoking of tobacco in railway carriages and elsewhere and the prevention of nuisances;
(*d*) with respect to the receipt and delivery of goods, and
(*e*) for regulating the passage of bicycles and other vehicles on footways and other premises controlled by the Boards, and intended for the use of those on foot.

(2) The Railways Board may make bylaws in relation to passengers and goods conveyed in or on ships operated by the Board, and as to their embarkation and disembarkation.

(3) Any bylaws made under this section may provide that any person contravening them shall be liable on summary conviction to a penalty not exceeding twenty-five pounds for each offence.'

Despite these legal supports for managerial authority the transport industry still has problems of how to achieve successful subordination.

If subordinates are not given a certain amount of authority to do things at their own discretion, little will be done. There are dangers in spreading authority in an organisation; but there are equal dangers in confining it too much. Few business organisations succeed in striking a balance. They are either over-centralised or too decentralised.

Protagonists of centralisation claim that it makes for strong management, and that strong management is needed for effective co-ordination of departments of organisation. Authority that is delegated alters the relative position of the superior. With every addition to the authority of a subordinate the superior becomes *relatively* weaker. On the other hand protagonists of decentralisation suggest that the head of a business is never wiser than a number of subordinates: two heads are always better than one. They see strength in the exercise of authority in accordance with the wisdom of many men, rather than that of any one fallible being.

Mr Kruschev supported strong government to prevent what he called 'the decay of the sense of overriding purpose'. A certain Chairman of a Nationalised Corporation is said to have brought to his undertaking 'authority and idealism'. Sufficiently strong authority must be exercised at the top, to control the authority that is created by delegation.

Authority may be given *expressly* in writing, with carefully prepared 'terms-of-reference', that clearly express its extent. For example, a manager may be authorised to engage and dismiss operatives; frame and issue instructions covering the operation and maintenance of his equipment; employ contractors if he judges it to be necessary; buy minor equipment up to items not exceeding £500 in value; dispose of equipment up to items not exceeding £100 in value; and so on. But authority may be added to *by default*. A subordinate takes it upon himself to exercise authority that has not been expressly given to him. If he is not checked he may presume a right to continue. And so a considerable amount of additional authority may grow up through a process of trial, which if successful may gain acceptance by custom and usage.

Indefinite authority is commonly created by establishing new 'levels', or steps, in the chain of command. The number of levels of authority in an organisation is some indication of the weight of authority that bears on operatives. Managements must give serious thought to what is the right number of levels of authority to have in their organisations. An organisation like the British

Transport Commission with its 730,000 employees could hardly avoid having a number of levels of authority. However, an organisation containing one million operatives with any one man controlling no more than ten subordinates would need only six levels of management.

Figures 17, 18 and 19 show the position of railway management in the organisational structure of the British Transport Commission in 1960.

(1) *The Commission*

(*a*) Primarily a policy-making body,

(*b*) Also supervised and co-ordinated divisional and area boards' activities,

(*c*) Retained complete authority in following matters:

(i) general financial control,

(ii) general commercial policy, tariffs, relations with important customers,

(iii) more important labour relations,

(iv) important dealings with government,

(v) senior appointments,

(vi) research,

(vii) design, construction and seaworthiness of ships, safety of life at sea and co-ordination of shipping services,

(viii) and the following railways matters: design, manufacture, procurement and standards of maintenance of locomotives, rolling stock, permanent way, signalling and some electrical equipment; policies and principles to be adopted in railway operation; overall control and allocation of rolling stock.

(2) *Committees*

Had executive power to deal with subjects of general concern (i.e. not peculiar to one Division). They were able to act on behalf of the Commission within certain limits. All the Committees affected railway management.

(3) *Sub-Commissions*

Did not have executive power—their role was in the nature of a liaison body. Nevertheless, one of the sub-committees affected railway management.

(4) *The Advisers (known collectively as General Staff)*

The Advisers were heads of the Departments shown. The Advisers, or General Staff, assisted the Commission in the transaction of their business and were the normal channels of communication between the Commission and the Area Boards of the railways, and the other divisions. All the Advisers affected the management of the railways.

(5) *The Departments*

Departments were required to seek authority from the General Staff only on matters of organisation, or on which they needed policy guidance. All the departments affected the management of the railways.

(6) *British Railways Central Staff*

The British Railways Central Staff were 'attached to' the General Staff and dealt specifically with certain railways subjects reserved to the Commission.

(7) *Divisions of the Commission*

Although British Railways was a Division of the Commission, it was not an entity having a Board of Management, like all the other Divisions (with the exception of the Road Passenger Services Divisions). Thus Area Boards came under single authority only in the person of the Chairman of the Commission. They were, however, partly subject to the many separate authorities described above.

(8) *Area Boards of British Railways*

Within the framework of the functions delegated to them the Area Boards were required to exercise overall direction of management within their Regions, but to leave day-to-day management to the Regional General Managers.

(9) *Railways Regions*

The railways regions were organisational units controlled by Area Boards. Each region was under a General Manager (Managing Director) responsible to an Area Board.

Thus, although British Railways was one of the seven divisions controlled by the Commission, there was no railways management at divisional level. The Area Boards were controlled directly by the Commission. British Railways Division

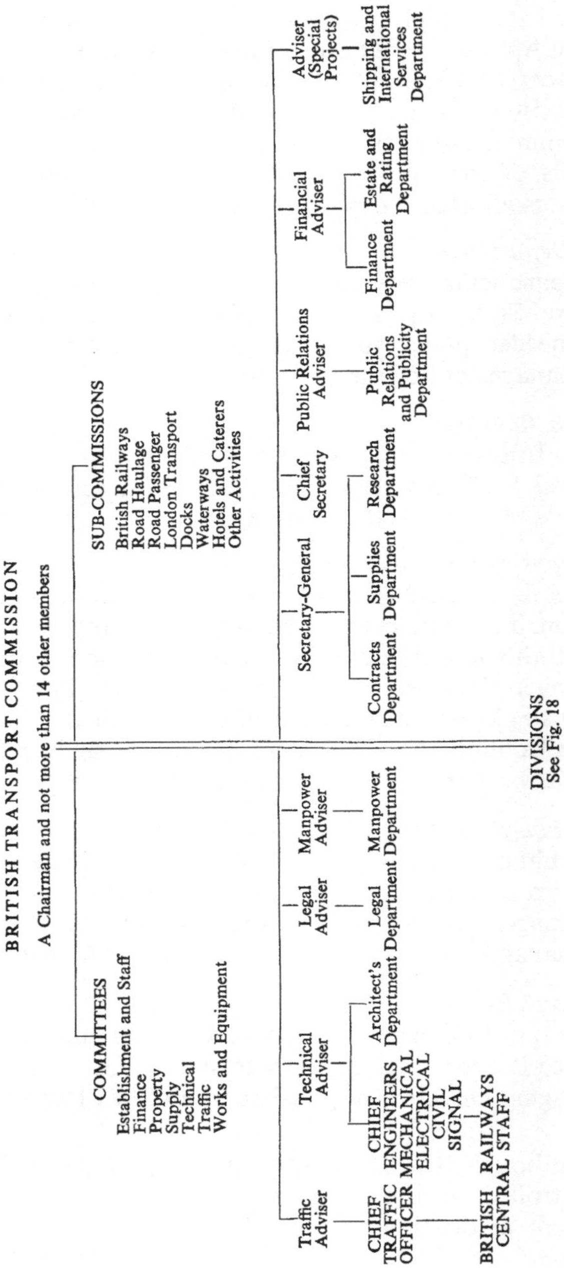

FIG. 17. *British Transport Commission—Headquarters Organisation (1960)*

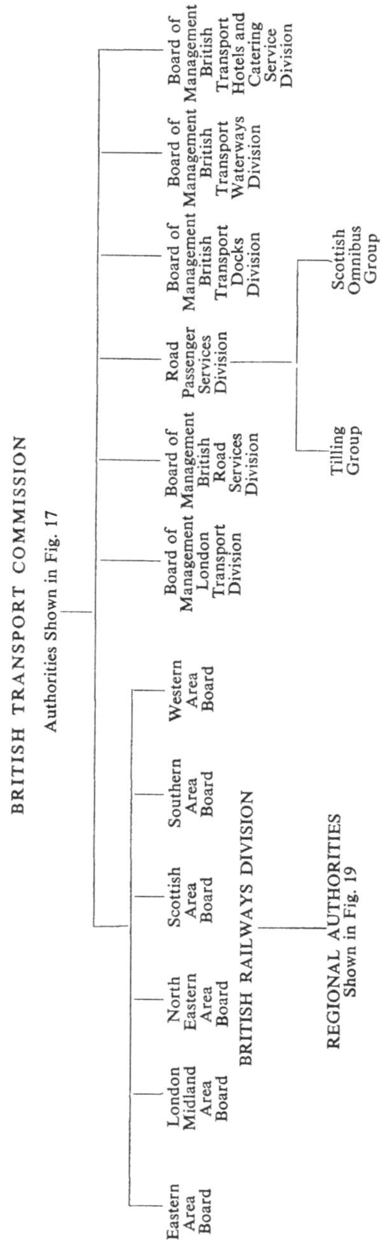

FIG. 18. *British Transport Commission—Outline Organisation of Divisions* (1960)

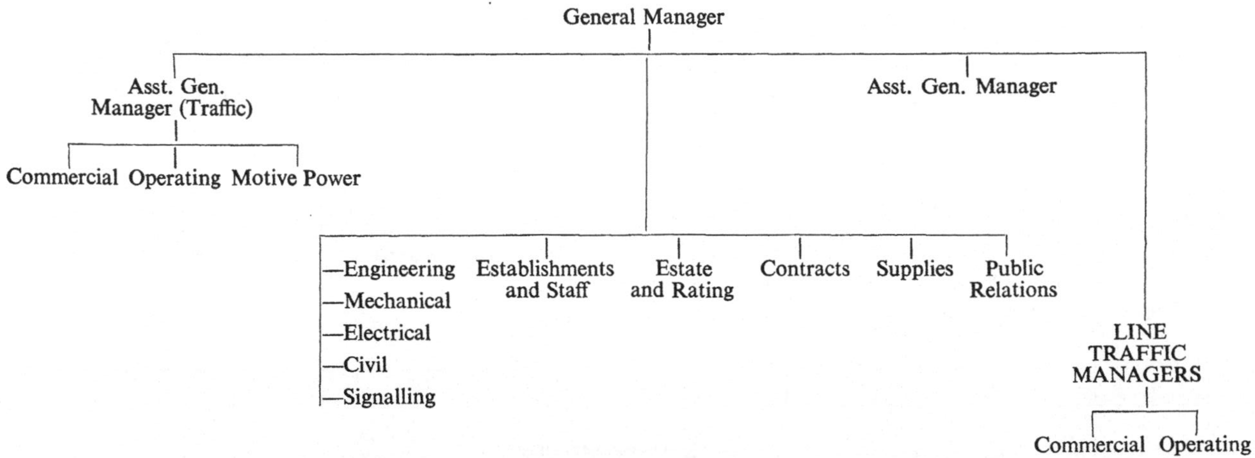

FIG. 19. *Typical Organisation of a Railways Region just before the passing of the Transport Act 1962*

N.B. Regional Traffic Departments were still in process of development, in accordance with Commission's policy of *decentralisation of management* to the 'men on the ground'.

existed more as an idea than a reality, as it had no separate management of its own.

The Select Committee on Nationalised Industries, in its Report on British Railways published in 1960, stated their belief 'that in fact a great field of decision had been devolved upon Area Boards by the Commission, and that there were good reasons for the *retention by the Commission* of the remaining powers'. Nearly half of British Railways' traffic crossed Area Boundaries, and rolling stock had to move anywhere in the system. This called for standardisation of equipment, stores, maintenance and training of staff. Top-grade technical staff, employed at a level above Area Boards, could be available for all Regions. Moreover the Commission, by controlling top appointments throughout Regions, prevented competition for scarce first-class men.

Standards of maintenance were laid down centrally, but the way in which these standards were achieved was left to the Regions. Earlier, centralised control over purchasing had been relaxed to a point where Regions were buying more than was the central buying department. The Commission laid down the standards for coaching stock, but allowed the Regions to decide upon their own interior décor.

On the commercial side Area Boards were allowed considerable freedom in fixing reduced fares, such as excursion fares, but they had very little authority to fix ordinary fares. Again, Area Boards had authority to quote special prices for freight in full-load wagons, but the Commission retained the authority to deal with the most important national customers.

The process of re-equipment threw interesting light on authority at various levels. General Managers of Regions were authorised to submit their own ideas to Area Boards, and *at the same time* submit the proposals to the staff at British Railways H.Q. (consisting of Chief Traffic Officer, Chief Mechanical Engineer, Chief Electrical Engineer, Chief Civil Engineer and Chief Signal Engineer). The Area Board was then authorised to approve, and to execute any scheme for re-equipment that did not cost more than £100,000.

The Select Committee reported that 'the Area Boards are, it seems, on the whole content with the limit of £100,000 put on the schemes which they may authorise', but that 'the Chairman of the Southern Area Board said that he himself found that the physical limitation of the work that could be done by his staff was more restricting than the limits placed on his expenditure'. On the other hand, it was noticeable that the Southern Region was slow in decentralising to line organisation.

Fig. 19 showing the typical organisation of a railways region just before the passing of the Transport Act 1962, reflects a reorganisation, designed to free the General Manager from much detail. This was done by subordinating the previous operating, commercial and motive power departments to the authority of an Assistant General Manager (Traffic). It was claimed that, by this means, the man who sold traffic was also responsible for seeing that the trains carrying it were available and running well. But, of course, it might be argued that what happened was this: the man who both provided and sold services was once the General Manager, and then an Assistant General Manager was added with authority to do the same job. The Commission's 1961 Report showed that the traffic organisation, which combined railways' commercial and operating activities under the Traffic Adviser (who also co-ordinated the traffic affairs of all the nationalised transport interests), had been reviewed 'with the aim of reducing the great load of work which these responsibilities placed on one individual'. As a result of this review, the Traffic Adviser's appointment had been abolished at the end of 1961, and the commercial and operating departments were separated, and placed under a Chief Commercial Officer and a Chief Operating Officer respectively. This appeared to be the reverse of what had previously gone on at Regional level. There it was argued that an *additional level* of authority was needed to *join* commercial and operating departments. But at Commission level it was argued that it was desirable to *remove a level* of authority in order to separate commercial and operating departments.

The numerous reorganisations, some integrating, some separating, some centralising, some decentralising, reflect the fundamental issues in attempts to subordinate successfully the elements of organisation. They reflect management's preoccupation with the principles of how much authority shall be passed on from the top to subordinate levels, and how many layers of authority there shall be. They reflect the search for the right answer to the question—what sort of authority and how much authority shall be established at each level? These are not matters that concern only the top men of a huge undertaking like the BTC. They are issues facing most managers of small organisations, whether they be independent or part of a large organisation.

The Transport Act 1962 swept away three great tiers of the British Transport Commission managerial superstructure. When the provisions of the Act came into force railway management began with a Railways Board, consisting of a chairman, a vice-chairman, or two vice-chairmen, and not more than sixteen nor less than ten other members. The Railways Board was required to set up six Regional Railway Boards to share among them responsibility for all parts of the national railway system. The Railways Board must, *in determining what functions are to be delegated by them*, act on lines settled from time to time with the approval of the Minister. This clause will, presumably, enable the Minister to step in and check what he may regard as excessive centralisation or decentralisation. We might assume that this question was considered to be of some importance in the eyes of the legislators.

The act of nationalisation resulted partly from certain premises concerning centralisation and decentralisation of authority. Critics of the privately-run railways companies said they had too much power to do just what they liked. It was argued that authority should be withdrawn from each 'part' of our national railways system, so that the parts could be compelled to co-operate with each other, and in the national interests. Many people said that too much authority was taken from the men on the spot, leaving them too weak to control and operate their railways. Others have said that the most serious defect of the mammoth British Transport Commission was that it failed to do the very thing it was set up to do, that is to exercise authority over the various parts of the railway system.

CHAPTER IX

ORGANISATIONAL GROUPS

There is a traditional view that the business of transport is based on the vehicle, the road and the load. We might then expect to find that the organisational groupings in the industry reflect the fundamental importance of these elements. A number of operatives are 'grouped' if they are linked by authority, to ensure co-operation. *Co-operation* is compelled by acts of *co-ordination.* Operatives may co-operate among themselves, but by definition authority is necessary to co-ordinate them. The *sine qua non* of an organisational group is that each individual is subject to the same overriding authority. For example, if Foreman A controls 20 operatives, Foreman B controls 20 operatives and Foreman C controls 20 operatives, we have three organisational groups. But these three groups may be contained within a larger group (see Fig. 20), again under a single overriding authority.

Where can we find a clear picture of what the organisational groups are, in the various types of transport undertakings? How useful, for example, was the British Transport Commission's classification of Staff (Fig. 21), contained in their Annual Report and Accounts? The tables presented a classification of people, according to the sort of work they were doing:

(1) Administrative, clerical and technical,
(2) Inspecting,
(3) Operating,
(4) Maintenance and construction,
(5) Power generating,
(6) Police,
(7) Miscellaneous.

The category of 'administrative, clerical and technical', included people in authority, and those assisting them in the

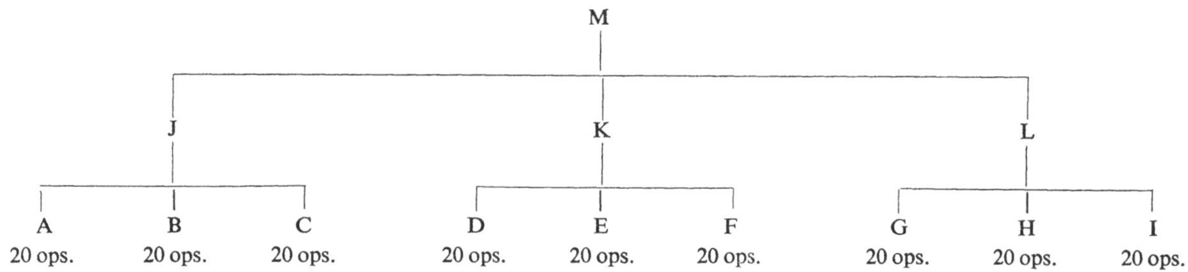

Foremen A, B and C report to Superintendent J: Foremen D, E and F report to Superintendent K: Foremen G, H and I report to Superintendent L. Each foreman has 20 operatives working for him. Superintendents J, K and L report to Manager M. There are thus 13 men in positions of authority and there are 13 organisational groups.

FIG. 20. *Showing How Organisational Groups are Defined*

Railways	Road Haulage	Road Passenger Services Provincial and Scottish	London Transport	Ships and Marine
Administrative Technical Clerical	Administrative and Clerical	Administrative and Clerical	Administrative Technical Clerical and Control	Administrative Technical Clerical
H.Q. and Inspectors				
Operating	Operating	Operating	Operating Railways Road	Operating
Maintenance and Construction	Maintenance	Maintenance	Mechanical Engineering Civil Engineering	Maintenance
Electrical Generating and Sub-station			Electrical Engineering	
Police				
Miscellaneous	Miscellaneous	Miscellaneous	Miscellaneous	Miscellaneous

FIG. 21. *British Transport Commission: Annual Report and*

exercise of authority. This was not an organisational group, but a mental classification. It suggested how much authority there was in the organisation.

The second category—those doing inspecting work—were the eyes and ears of management. And we will often find that they are the eyes and ears of *senior* management. They do sometimes form an organisational group. Inspectors may be gathered together into an inspection branch, but in other cases inspectors may be attached to local units. Whether or not inspectors are placed in their own organisational group may be decided by the need for them to be able to stand up to managerial authority. For example, inspectors of accounts, are usually grouped together in an Internal Audit Branch that has authority independent of that of the Chief Accountant.

Operating people, according to the classification used by the BTC (Fig. 22) were:

Inland Waterways	Docks Harbours and Wharves	Hotels and Catering	Head Office
Administrative Technical Clerical	Administrative Technical Clerical	H.Q. Area Administrative and Clerical	Administration
			Attendants
		Hotels	Training Operational Research
Operating	Operating		Secretariats
		Refreshment Rooms	Estate and Rating
Maintenance	Maintenance		Research Design Archives
		Restaurant Cars	Supplies Contracts Paper and Printing
			Films
			Police Legal
Miscellaneous	Miscellaneous	Common Services	Commercial Advertising

Accounts: Categories Shown in Statistics of Staff for Various Divisions

(*a*) those who worked at stations and depots, dealing with passengers and freight.

N.B.: Some of those classified as operating were persons in authority, e.g. stationmasters and yardmasters. The Administrative class already referred to were people who exercised authority from Headquarters.

(*b*) those who worked on vehicles, carrying passengers and freight.

The word 'operating' derives from a root that means 'to work'. Operating people are working people. It may seem strange for any single group to refer to themselves as *the* working people, but sometimes people in operating groups believe they are the people who do 'the real work of the business'. Is there any justification for this attitude?

The proper effect of a transport undertaking is to secure the

British Railways	Road Haulage	Road Passenger Services
(*a*) Stationmasters, yardmasters, goods agents Inspectors, foremen and supervisors Traffic Control Drivers, motormen, firemen and cleaners Guards, signalmen, shunters, porters and ticket collectors Goods and cartage Locomotive running shed Carriage and wagon cleaners, examiners, etc. Machinery and water softening plant attendants	Supervisors Traffic Clerks Drivers Mates Van guards Loaders Yardmen	Supervisors Drivers Conductors
(*b*) Foremen, inspectors and other Supervisors Civil engineering Signal and telecommunications Locomotive Carriage and wagon Locomotive running shed Electrical, road motor, stores and miscellaneous	Supervisors Clerks Mechanized Maintenance Stores	Supervisors Mechanical Maintenance in (*a*) Shop (*b*) Garage Building Maintenance

FIG. 22. *British Transport Commission Staff*

arrival of people and goods at destinations of choice. Operating groups—those at terminals and in vehicles—are thus at the heart of the carrier business. They are the people who are closest to carrying out the real intention of the business. A transport system is partly an inert, costly mass of materials that must be brought to life to earn their keep. All ranks are rightly infused with the idea that every day a ship spends in dock costs the company so much, or that every hour an aircraft spends on the ground costs the airline so much money. And the operating people are those who bring the whole system to life. This, however, is no good reason for regarding themselves as more important than other groups in business, because society will not permit them to carry out this simple intention without their doing a number of other jobs, such as keeping proper accounts, doing scheduled maintenance of their vehicles and so on.

The classification of staff into operating groups has some relevance to organisational groupings, as we shall see in more detail later. It is based upon raw materials and equipment.

London Transport	Ships and Marine	Inland Waterways	Docks Harbours and Wharves
Supervisors Motormen and drivers and conductors Guards Booking clerks Porters, ticket collectors	Ship's officers Stewards and catering Seamen and engine room Marine staff ashore	Supervisors Lock-keepers Bridge-keepers Reservoir attendants Warehouse, wharf and depot men Boatmen	Supervisors Railway Coal tipping and trimming Cranage loading and discharging in dock areas Docking and berthing Tugs and other floating craft
Supervisors Mechanical engineering, shop, garage and depot Civil engineering Railways—permanent way and signals Railways and road structures Shops Repair work	Supervisors Marine workshops	Supervisors Engineering Boat-builders and repairers Dredgermen	Supervisors Engineering Artisan Labouring Dredging

Classified as (a) Operating, (b) Maintenance

Those in the maintenance and construction category were the people who repaired, replaced and modified equipment. Because maintenance is not primarily what the business exists for, management are usually ready to consider suggestions that maintenance can be done more cheaply by a contractor. The accounts of many carriers show costs of chartering crews and vehicles, far outweighed by contracting costs for maintenance and construction. Construction costs include the annual depreciation of equipment. Classification of staff under maintenance and construction has some relevance to organisational groupings in the industry. Maintenance people's raw materials are equipment (vehicles, track and terminals). Maintenance organisational groups are based on types of raw materials and probably, additionally, upon the equipment used on the raw materials, e.g. welding equipment, radio equipment, etc.

Power generating groups are organisational groups based on the use of very specialised equipment and raw materials. Similarly, the police are a logically based organisational group.

Titles of people in authority give us some idea of the bases of organisational groupings. Operatives and equipment in all stationmasters' groups do much the same work, but different from that of groups working in, say, maintenance sheds. Each stationmaster's group differs from other stationmasters' groups by locality. The same is true of yardmasters' groups. Organisational groups headed by goods agents, have a particular type of raw material, that they specialise in handling. Inspectors in the operating group also specialise in particular facets of the working of railway operatives and equipment. Foremen and supervisors probably represent the oldest, simplest, but still the most important basis of division of operatives—into *manageable groups*.

There were some similarities between the staff classifications of the predecessor of the four nationalised British Transport Boards, and those of the British air corporations. The 'operations' classification was used, for example, by BOAC (Fig. 23), but the category was more restricted; it included vehicle staff only. The definition had been narrowed considerably to exclude all ground staff, and was demonstrated by the description 'Flight' Operations. Some of the other world airlines put station staff in the category of 'Ground Operations'. The route organisation (excluding sales) was the station operation side of BOAC, but the groupings emphasised the geographical spread of airline organisation. The Engineering Department included maintenance, and what might be called in the airline business—reconstruction. It also included the development function. Significantly the airline proclaimed the existence of a selling group. That was a big difference between the airlines and the divisions of the BTC. The former believed they had to sell hard; the latter did not believe this was necessary. The Finance and Properties, and Non-departmental branches of BOAC were equivalent to the Administrative and Clerical groups of the surface transport undertakings.

The problems of making the best organisational groups in transport undertakings are illustrated by the position of the railways in the late 1950's and early 1960's. The major groupings below Commission Headquarters were regional. Theoretically regional groupings gathered together operatives, equipment and raw materials that were within certain area boundaries, fashioned for ease of communication and control. The regional groupings

APPENDIX 25 TO REPORT FROM THE SELECT COMMITTEE ON NATIONALISED INDUSTRIES. (REPORTS AND ACCOUNTS)—THE AIR CORPORATIONS

1. *Flight Operations Department*
   (*a*) Operational
      (1) Flight Deck
      (2) Cabin Crews
   (*b*) Non-operational

2. *Engineering Department*
   Hourly-rated
   Supervisory
   Supplies
   Technical Administration

3. *Routes Organisation* (*excluding Sales*)
   UK
   Overseas

4. *Selling*

5. *Finance and Properties*
   Finance and Accounts
   Property and Services

6. *Non-Departmental*
   Secretary and Legal
   Press and Information
   Personnel
   Restaurant and Canteens
   Medical

FIG. 23. *Breakdown of Corporation strength* (*B O A C*)

of the railways were not geographically logical and many of them had eccentricities due to historical accident.

Each regional group was controlled by a General Manager. The sub-group regarded as the most important within each regional group was called the Traffic Department, controlled by an Assistant General Manager. Finance, Engineering (Mechanical, Electrical, Civil and Signalling), Establishments and Staff, Estate and Rating, Contracts, Supplies and Public Relations were regarded as less important sub-groups, and were controlled by Departmental Officers. Organisation varied somewhat from region to region, because the elements of organisation were not the same in each. For example, the major raw materials of the Southern Region were passengers, whereas those of the London Midland Region were freight. But generally Traffic Departments grouped organisational elements concerned in the work of three departments of the former railway companies: commercial, operating and motive power.

The Commission had not prescribed regional organisation, but had laid down a policy of decentralisation of management to the 'men on the ground'. This phrase, 'men on the ground', was an official utterance of the Commission, and it was significant in the story of groupings and regroupings. Groups had tended to be formed around particular types of equipment or raw material. There were vehicle groups, station groups, railway-track groups, passenger groups, goods groups, and so on. These groups were not compelled to co-operate and sometimes left the man who had to put passengers and goods into vehicles, and run vehicles along the track, unable to do the job. The 'men on the ground' were at the point where many *organisational* groups based on equipment and raw materials had to come together to do a single *business* job: the job of securing the arrival of passengers or freight.

Men who are organised around a particular piece of equipment are likely to become technically efficient in the use of it. Men organised around a particular type of raw material are likely to become expert in the handling of it. But, when we get away from simple divisions aimed at making 'manageable' groups, and divide by type of equipment or raw material, we may weaken the authority of general business management. This is the dilemma, particularly in transport undertakings: certain groupings make for the efficiency of specialist organisations but weaken the authority of general business management. Certain groupings make for strong authority of general management, but lower technical standards. Organisations continually reshuffle organisation groups in search of the optimum position.

The Eastern Region was the first to produce a regrouping to strengthen the authority of the men on the ground. They created three sub-groups based on three original lines of which it was principally composed: Great Northern; Great Eastern; London,

Tilbury and Southend. Each line was controlled by a Line Traffic Manager, who reported directly to the General Manager. The General Manager's traffic groups were to be similar to those at regional headquarters, so that each Line Manager would have both operating and commercial groups under his authority. Below the Line Managers there were District Traffic Managers; four on the Great Northern line, three on the Great Eastern line, and one on the London, Tilbury and Southend line.

At the same time the Commission were asking regions to 'streamline' their technical organisations and to achieve 'a measure of uniformity'. Firstly, they were pressing regions to ensure that at depot level, the man who operated the trains also kept them in running order. This was a clear illustration that, at certain levels, organisational groups must take account of the whole purpose of the business. Business must not be frustrated by its own organisation.

And this is what bad groupings of the elements of organisation can do. They can destroy authority where it is important to have it, and destroy a sense of business purpose.

Secondly, the Commission were asking regions to bring Mechanical, Electrical and Carriage and Wagon Engineering into one organisational group. It was thought that at regional level these should not be reporting to the General Manager as separate groups.

The regional groupings themselves were closely examined in 1962, and in September of that year two changes were announced to speed up business and unify management. Organisational groupings had been faulty business instruments, and had impaired authority by splitting management. A part of the Western Regional group was handed over to the London Midland Regional group. A part of the Southern Regional group was handed over to the Western Regional group. Since nationalisation in 1947 two groups (Western and London Midland) had been operating in Birmingham and the Black Country. Both the Southern and Western Regional groups had operated in Exeter, and in an area west of Exeter.

In an illustration of the organisational structure of a typical medium-sized bus company (Fig. 24) it will be seen that a finance group has been given higher status. The finance group was highly placed in our airline illustration, but was in a sub-

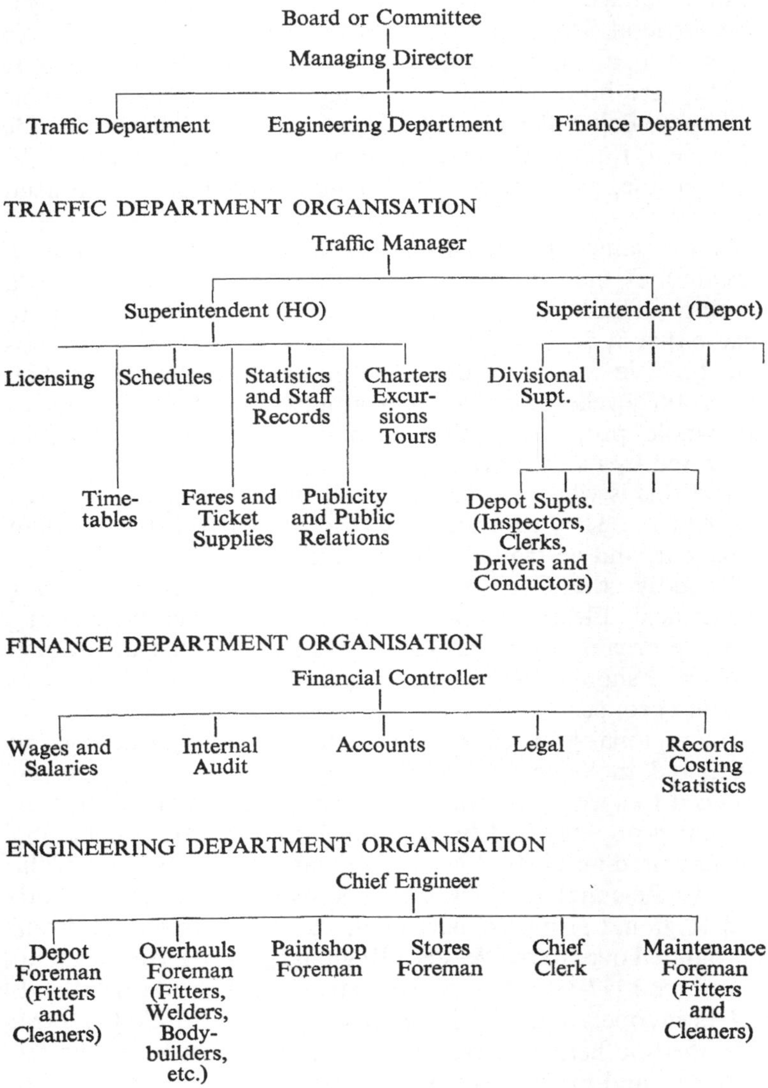

FIG. 24. *Organisational Groups in a Typical Medium-sized Bus Company*

ordinate role in the BTC illustrations, and obscured by the label of 'administrative and clerical'. In the bus company the major groupings of Traffic and Engineering closely resembled the major groupings of Operating and Maintenance discussed earlier. There were strong arguments in some companies as to whether drivers should be in the engineering group or the traffic group. Drivers and conductors both came under the traffic manager, on the ground that vehicle staff should not be divided by membership of separate organisation groups. Separate groupings meant two sets of rosters and liaison work to match the rosters. Two sets of investigators were necessary if anything went wrong, and at the end of them divergent penalties might result.

Chief Engineers argued that drivers were handling expensive pieces of equipment, and the way they handled them could profoundly affect maintenance costs, so they ought to be regarded as engineers. Broadly similar discussions are provoked by placing airline cabin staff in the traffic group and flight deck staff in an operations group.

Few divisions are so clear-cut that they eliminate all traces of the illogical; they all leave some room for bickering among the heads of groups. If only we could destroy the managerial pride that breeds on larger and larger organisational groups! But as it is an accountant doing costing in a maintenance shop may be 'claimed' by chief accountant or chief engineer. An electrician, working in a mechanical maintenance shop, might be claimed by both Electrical and Mechanical Chief Engineers. Vehicle cleaners at stations may just as logically become part of a station group or a maintenance group.

Is there any principle on which to resolve conflicting views? Certainly there is no ready-made answer, applicable to all circumstances. But sound judgements call for an awareness of the issues involved, which are:

(*a*) technical efficiency—which is usually promoted by specialists working in specialist groups,
(*b*) authority—which is usually promoted by strong co-ordination of specialists to ensure they all work to the same end.

The needs of authority should not be sacrificed to those of technical efficiency. The latter is a means to an end, and is worthless if it does not serve the ends of business. The bases of organisational groups found in transport undertakings may be summarised as follows. These groups are not mutually exclusive, nor is there a wholly consistent pattern of bases for either major or minor groups.

1. Specialist management groups: finance, purchasing, production (operating and maintenance), marketing, development, personnel, etc.
2. Operating groups to include all parts of organisation engaged in moving traffic. (Operating groups are sometimes called Traffic Groups.)
3. Specialist operating groups: flight, ground, passenger and goods traffic.
4. Maintenance groups to include all parts of organisation engaged in repair and overhaul of equipment.
5. Specialist maintenance groups: electrical, mechanical, civil, signalling, radio, etc.
6. Power generating groups.
7. Selling (or commercial) groups.
8. Regional groups based on elements of organisation contained within a small area such as a passenger station, or goods depot, or covering a wide area such as a country.

CHAPTER X

THE HUMAN ELEMENT IN THE ORGANISATION OF A TRANSPORT BUSINESS

There are traditions in the transport industry. The behaviour of captain and crew of a sinking liner will probably be influenced by long-established custom. So will the attitude of the crew of a ship that has received a call for assistance from a vessel in distress. Recurring stories of gallantry and self-sacrifice in the face of danger tell us of beliefs and practices, handed on from generation to generation.

Traditions are not confined to seafaring, nor do they always involve spectacular feats. A tradition of reliability was nourished in stage-coach services at the end of the eighteenth century: 'getting through with the mail' soon became a matter of honour. Today transport men are reluctant to cancel a service, or abandon a journey. It is apparent to the private motorist, accustomed to the manners of his fellows, that drivers of heavy transport lorries have a different attitude to driving. The courtesy and responsibility that distinguish these relative newcomers to the industry, are already rooted in traditions that bind a multitude of carriers in a companionship of the road. Train-drivers still do everything within their power to be on time. Pilots of air ambulances will strain every nerve to get patients to hospital as comfortably and as quickly as possible.

What lies behind such attitudes so altruistic in a commercial or industrial setting? Customers and general public become deeply involved in the industry's production process. Those in the industry acquire a sense of responsibility from being aware of this fact. When a customer commits himself or his goods to a carrier, he is very trusting. Transport men at scenes of disaster usually show feelings of having betrayed that trust. But it does not need a disaster to make transport operatives recognise their responsibilities to passengers or shippers. They seldom need to be reminded that a trainload of passengers is a trainload of people, to whom it is important to arrive somewhere, on time. Even if it is only to get the kids to the seaside, with their buckets and spades for the day, it is important. Crews of cargo vessels are aware of the importance of the food or medical supplies, or whatever it is, they carry. Transport men recognise that their service is a lifeline between one community and another.

This recognition brings to the work of transport operatives, a sense of purpose—almost of importance. They are not worried by feelings that beset workers in many occupations—that of doing something trivial, or even something that is likely to damage the health and happiness of the consumer.

Another factor contributing to the development of traditions among operatives in transport, is the challenging nature of the overall task. The task of carrying people and goods from one place to another is a struggle against the forces of nature. Beginning with the initial effort needed to overcome inertia, the carrier continues to combat geographical 'controls' of distance, physical features (mountains, desert, sea, etc.), and climate (winds, precipitation, storms, etc.). Transport has changed the significance of these controls. Not long ago the distance between London and Sydney was 35 days; now the same distance may be reckoned as 42 hours. Until recently the Atlantic Ocean presented an impassible barrier between Europe and the American Continent. Until recently the Sahara Desert was a barrier to commerce between peoples of the North African littoral and those of the Equatorial Region. Yet, in spite of these triumphs, transport systems are still endangered by natural elements, from icy roads that cause buses to skid off highways, to storms at sea that still sink ships. There is no perfectly safe system of transport, and there probably never will be. Safety must be bought at the price of constant vigilance.

There is enthusiasm among operatives in the industry. We are still not surprised to hear service at sea referred to as a 'calling', or that the sea is in people's blood, or that it runs in families. Service on railways has long evoked similar feelings. Through father and son there has developed an almost sentimental regard for locomotives. And it is the same with aircraft.

There are many men who are unhappy away from the smell of aircraft; even declining promotion to remain with them.

For one reason or another there is a considerable influence for good, generated in the industry. Unfortunately management has occasionally taken advantage of traditional conduct and natural enthusiasm, to avoid giving operatives decent working conditions. Managers have to learn to use good morale for the benefit of the industry and the community it serves.

We may classify production operatives into two categories: (*a*) those handling vehicles, and (*b*) those dealing with customers. Those handling vehicles may be divided into (i) people directing or guiding vehicles, and (ii) people maintaining vehicles. Those dealing with customers may be divided into (i) those dealing with passengers, and (ii) those dealing with shippers of goods, and the goods themselves. Skilled operatives in these groups are the most likely to require characteristics special to the transport industry.

The endowments required by staff directing or guiding vehicles vary with the complexity of vehicles and the particular techniques associated with them. But usually a man's physique must at least be able to sustain a consistently good performance. For example, consistent performance must not be impaired by defective vision or hearing. Secondly, the individual must usually be capable of bearing the physical strain of emergencies. He must not suffer from any disease that might render him ineffective at a moment's notice. We are less certain about general intelligence. Because so little work has been done to find the optimum level for various vehicle operatives, errors in selection have to be corrected by eliminating people who lack the intelligence to complete their training.

Managers concerned with getting people of the right intelligence would be well advised to keep records of the general intelligence of all their vehicle operatives, and match these findings against performance on the job. At the moment guesswork is leading some managers to demand higher and higher academic attainments, as a kind of insurance policy.

The verbal facility of vehicles operatives must be adequate to deal with study media and communications. Ability to use numbers is important in the handling of ships and aircraft, and there are obvious advantages in staff having mechanical ability.

Most managers, in talking of the disposition they require of their vehicle operatives, use words like methodical, cautious, persistent, and so on. They almost all, at some time, refer to 'a sense of duty'. Duty is something that one ought or is bound to do. A sense of duty is particularly important in transport because of shifts or watches. Duty officers, or officers of a watch, without a sense of duty may be tempted to evade responsibility. Many managers claim that a sense of duty is more important than intelligence. This is debatable, but we must accept it as a proper emphasis on sense of duty. The amount of skill required of vehicle operatives again depends upon the complexity of the vehicle, its associated techniques, its speed, rate and quantity of communications. It also depends upon the geographical controls exerted on the vehicle, upon the consequence of accidents and upon the concomitant social and political responsibilities. It is very difficult to judge the amount of knowledge vehicle operatives require to sustain their skill. Probably managements demand too much just to be on the safe side. Management must have the courage not to overburden vehicle operatives, to avoid the remotest chance of blame on themselves in the event of an accident. With knowledge, as with the other characteristics, management should draw up a clear specification of what they require.

Operatives concerned with maintaining vehicles may not need such exceptional standards of physique, or general intelligence, or verbal facility, but they require higher than average number and mechanical facility. They should be thoroughly reliable in disposition. They must have a sense of duty as marked as that of vehicle operatives. Again, the skill of maintenance men should be related to the complexity of the vehicle. Electrical equipment may require more skill than mechanical equipment, or electronic equipment may require more skill than electrical equipment. Of course, this is an over-simplification as there is very complicated mechanical equipment and very simple electrical equipment. A highly developed skill is that of diagnosing faults in unserviceable equipment and in certifying that equipment is in sound running order. The former can save money by reducing the time taken to find out what is wrong; the latter is at the root of safe operation. Wide knowledge is needed to sustain diagnostic skill and, generally, it is desirable to specialise and conserve the skill.

The physique of operatives dealing with customers may be important from the marketing point of view. In general it is better if operatives who deal with customers have an attractive, rather than repelling appearance, and that they are not subject to frightening ailments. They should at least possess enough common sense to match up to the average customer. Verbal facility can be very important where there is an urgent need to explain, guide or persuade. Numerical facility may be important in the calculation of fares. Mechanical facility is not so important as for operatives handling vehicles. People dealing with customers should be disposed to do things for other people, and to be cheerful, energetic and gifted with endurance. Their skills are the social skills of 'getting on with people', and of not angering them at every turn. Knowledge should be wider than it usually is with these people. They may be asked a very wide range of questions. They are the bridge between the customer and a complicated production process. They are also the people who have the vital role of seeing that the customer plays a helpful part in the production process.

Training presents some particular problems in a transport business. Skill is established by eliminating wrong actions and developing correct movements into habit. Training must be long enough to form habits. Lengthy training in classrooms is very costly, so policy must provide for as much as possible to be done on the job. Supervisors are in the best position to instill correct habits among operatives.

Mechanical tasks usually lend themselves to some form of simulation, for training purposes. The difficulty is with environmental factors. For example, there is no real substitute for route or line experience for the vehicle operative. Many operative licences will not be issued on the strength of a training course without experience on the line. In transport, as in many other industries, experience is the great teacher.

Another characteristic problem is that of persuading operatives to rely on the feedbacks they receive from instruments. This is particularly so in the case of vehicle operatives, who direct their vehicles visually in clear visibility, and find it difficult to ignore sensory impressions in bad visibility. A pilot's senses frequently delude him as to direction and position, and he has to make a conscious effort to maintain belief in his instruments. Faith in instruments is something that comes from considerable experience of their reliability, and it cannot be gained in classrooms.

Part of the problem of training for safety is to encourage constant vigilance. Unfortunately the training situation in this respect is inherently unstable. Alertness eliminates accidents, and the absence of accidents lulls minds into a sense of security. At certain road junctions major accidents vary in inverse proportion with the number of minor accidents. Many people have experienced the peculiar dangers of 'safe' motorways. Their lack of danger is monotonous and has a soporific effect that can destroy judgement and bring disaster. Eventless journeys are not sufficiently challenging. The training problem is to keep people alive *to the dangers of safety.*

There is a similar problem in the training of maintenance workers. Failsafe systems tend to promote a sense of infallibility. Operatives know that if one instrument fails there is a standby, or that if one power system fails the operator can switch over to another. This knowledge may take the edge off a worker's conscientiousness. Maintenance workers must be made to understand that the premise, on which failsafe systems work, is the reliability of *all parts*. The chances of standby parts failing as well as the original part must be small.

A special problem is the need for persistent drilling of operatives. They have to play their part, in what must inevitably be one of the most highly disciplined business organisations. They must obey regulations, and follow laid-down procedures to the letter. Yet their initiative must not be destroyed so that they are incapable of dealing with the unforeseen, or of assuming authority later in their careers. The severity of their training must be tempered by education.

The amount of effort that management has to put into training its operatives is related to the effort put into selection. Sometimes training has to remedy faults that a selection procedure has failed to reveal. Sometimes a training department asks for unskilled people. Training people may say that they prefer to teach somebody who knows nothing about a subject. This makes sense only if the alternative is someone who has been taught badly.

Generally managers need to study the human characteristics required of various operatives more carefully. Then, by careful selection, they can reduce training. As it is managers tend to play safe, by taking the best recruits they can get, according to the frequently irrelevant indicator of academic attainment. This can create artificial shortages for employers, and in the end cause dissatisfaction to operatives whose endowments are misemployed.

Even efficient selection procedures, and good training programmes, sometimes fail to produce operatives capable of doing certain jobs. There are limits beyond which human beings cannot be fitted to organisation, and then something must be done to fit organisation to human beings. In transport organisation the position may be reached at some points where the human element cannot be expected to adapt any further. A business organisation can become inhuman, and then it can no longer accommodate the human element. Then one of three things must happen. Business must stop: organisation must be humanised: or organisation must be changed to reduce the human element, and go over to automation.

A business can become inhuman in a number of ways. Ill-intentioned managers may over-reach themselves in efforts to get as much work as possible out of operatives. Or managers may thoughtlessly, or in ignorance of human limitations, allow faulty equipment design to increase the difficulty of work until it is beyond the capabilities of average human beings. An increasing amount of equipment is so complex in design, or exacting to operate, that human beings find it difficult to work with.

Part of the task of maintaining the human element in organisation lies in keeping operatives up to date with changes in procedure, equipment design and methods of operating. Technical progress has been exceptionally rapid in air transport, but important changes have been occurring in all branches of transport.

Finally we must note the particular difficulties in the transport industry of controlling people who are spread geographically (in stations and vehicles) or spread in time (on shifts or watches). It is difficult to obtain the normal managerial feedbacks from operatives, inaccessible for considerable periods of time. Inspectors may partly overcome this handicap, but no inspection can compensate for ill-disposed employees. Right disposition among transport employees is management's best guarantee of good service. Managers must inculcate a sense of duty into the human beings who answer to them.

SECTION II—INDUSTRIAL RELATIONS

CHAPTER XI

INDUSTRIAL RELATIONS IN THE TRANSPORT INDUSTRY

The relations between management and operatives have been extensively formalised in what are now usually called 'industrial relations'. These formal relations are centred on issues concerned with the essential 'act of exchange' that is involved in working for a business. The employee exchanges a certain amount of work for a certain amount of money. The exchange may be carefully regulated in quality of work and working conditions, but essentially it is the exchange of work for money. Industrial relations are based on economic considerations. They are materialist. For this reason many people have taken great pains to emphasise that they are not the whole story of the relations between management and operatives.

There is a danger that people will think that formal industrial relations are the only relations that matter. They may then neglect the day-to-day, on-the-job working relationships of managers and operatives that involve considerations other than the purely economic, for example, leadership and morale. Industrial relations, it is true, do not include on-the-job working relations. Industrial relations are formalised in this sense. They are channelled through representatives; they are not direct relations between the individual manager and the individual operative. Each has his mouthpiece—mouthpieces inside the business and outside the business. Spokesmen appear in all but the smallest businesses; and outside, the press, political parties, trade unions and employers' associations are all aligned on one side or the other. They are relations conducted within meetings, pre-arranged, minuted and run to a set of rules. Discussions outside these formal meetings are often frowned upon.

Collective bargaining is the central act of industrial relations. Collective bargaining prevents employers exploiting the weaknesses of individual workers, and prevents employers competing unfairly by such exploitation. Its founders saw it as a means of settling disputes without the need for strikes and lock-outs. Ideally this would be achieved by obtaining the consent of disputants, to a course of action that would be accepted voluntarily and loyally. The 'machinery' is a series of formalities, or processes, or procedures through which parties to a dispute will go, in order to settle it. The premise is that the procedures are inherently conciliatory. Even if the *machinery of conciliation* should fail the other half of the industrial relations equipment—the *arbitration machinery*—can be brought in to finish the job. Many Joint Industrial Councils (widely-used title for collective-bargaining machinery), when conciliation fails, refer their disputes to an arbitrator. The Industrial Court, set up under the Industrial Court Act 1919, appoints arbitrators. The Minister of Labour may appoint arbitrators under the same Act. Or Joint Industrial Councils may provide their own arbitration machinery.

Much of the idealism behind industrial relations machinery, owes its origin to the recommendations of a famous committee called the Whitley Committee. Whitley was the chairman of a Committee on the relations between Employers and Employed set up by the Government in 1916. The Committee recommended extending the practice of employers and employed *negotiating* wages and working conditions, to employers and employed *consulting* over the whole field of business, by:

'the establishment for each industry of an organisation, representative of employers and workpeople, to have as its object the regular consideration of matters affecting the progress and well-being of the trade from the point of view of all those engaged in it, so far as this is consistent with the general interests of the community'.

In negotiating wages and working conditions the aim is to

obtain agreement. The procedure is designed to that end, and if agreement is not obtained by negotiating (as collective bargaining is usually called) then agreement is obtained by both parties accepting the decision of an arbitrator. The whole point of the machinery is that it is a method of obtaining agreement. And it is a method that offers an alternative to strikes and lock-outs. Consultation does not have the same objective. In consultation, agreement is not the primary aim. The benefits of consultation can be obtained even if the parties 'consulting' end their discussions with different views. It is the wise course of management hearing the views of all interested parties before finally deciding and embarking on courses of action. Consultation was expected to be altruistic and to be a stage removed from the self-interest that naturally dominated negotiations. Thus—

'a permanent improvement in the relations between employers and employed must be founded upon something other than a cash basis. What is wanted is that the workpeople should have a greater opportunity of participating in the discussion about and adjustment of those parts of industry by which they are most affected.'

There is no reason for doubting the sincerity of those who wrote these words.

'We venture to hope that representative men in each industry, with pride in their calling and care for its place as a contributor to the national well-being, will come together in the manner here suggested, and apply themselves to promoting industrial harmony and efficiency and removing the obstacles that have hitherto stood in the way.'

Figures 25 and 26 from the Ministry of Labour's Industrial Relations Handbook illustrate that there has not been the steady decline in the use made of strikes, that was expected from post-war developments in negotiation and consultation. Workpeople are still preoccupied with pay and working conditions.

Although this cannot bring much comfort to those who looked for the disappearance of strikes, at least there is no evidence that *consultation* adds to the disputes. The fact that the causes shown are almost wholly pay and working conditions

*Industrial analysis of aggregate number of working days lost in all stoppages of work through industrial disputes in progress in the United Kingdom between 1949 and 1959 inclusive**

Industry Group†	Working days lost (thousands) in the years shown below										
	1949	1950	1951	1952	1953	1954	1955	1956	1957	1958	1959
Agriculture, Forestry, Fishing	11	43	1	4	—	‡	37	‡	5	1	‡
Coal Mining	754	431	350	660	393	468	1,112	502	514	450	363
Other Mining and Quarrying	1	‡	1	2	1	‡	‡	1	‡	‡	8
Treatment of Non-Metalliferous Mining Products	3	2	4	4	6	4	48	2	30	2	5
Chemicals and Allied Trades	2	6	1	7	1	6	15	5	‡	‡	73
Metal Manufacture	45	52	29	31	100	46	24	242	437	35	71
Shipbuilding and Ship Repairing	125	53	73	87	206	521	122	324	2,328	336	314
Engineering	52	50	137	185	566	48	67	77	2,716	74	99
Vehicles	60	132	266	468	589	99	439	362	868	161	465
Other Metal Industries	7	7	9	20	64	27	17	13	244	4	14
Textiles	68	4	8	2	19	3	15	28	37	10	54
Leather, etc.	13	1	—	‡	1	—	‡	‡	‡	—	‡
Clothing	9	3	8	3	8	9	8	1	7	10	2
Food, Drink and Tobacco	3	26	19	9	7	3	2	1	4	19	10
Manufactures of Wood and Cork	26	16	9	23	10	9	17	5	6	10	5
Paper and Printing	5	205	2	40	‡	19	73	371	1	4	3,509
Other Manufacturing Industries	17	3	7	16	16	30	7	17	34	5	7
Building and Contracting	31	64	83	157	101	233	71	78	84	151	138
Gas, Electricity and Water	36	42	62	11	1	3	‡	8	1	5	5
Transport, etc.	533	188	601	32	69	919	1,687	34	998	2,116	95
Distributive Trades	2	40	10	23	23	4	8	6	91	67	4
Other Services	4	21	14	8	3	6	12	6	7	2	29
Total	**1,807**	**1,389**	**1,694**	**1,792**	**2,184**	**2,457**	**3,781**	**2,083**	**8,412**	**3,462**	**5,270**

* The statistics relate to stoppages of work due to disputes connected with terms of employment or conditions of work. They exclude stoppages involving fewer than 10 workers and those which lasted less than one day, except any in which over 100 working days were lost.
† The industries have been classified in accordance with the 1948 edition of the Standard Industrial Classification.
‡ Less than 500 working days.

FIG. 25

Analysis of stoppages of work in the United Kingdom due to industrial disputes, by the principal cause of each stoppage beginning between 1949 and 1959 inclusive

Principal Cause of Disputes leading to a Stoppage of Work	Number of Stoppages beginning in years shown below										
	1949	1950	1951	1952	1953	1954	1955	1956	1957	1958	1959
Wages:—											
Claims for increases	83	78	190	115	97	116	196	286	327	224	238
Other wage disputes	528	509	643	611	694	811	1,035	922	952	984	730
All wage disputes	**611**	**587**	**833**	**726**	**791**	**927**	**1,231**	**1,208**	**1,279**	**1,208**	**968**
Hours of labour	54	37	37	58	45	47	45	74	117	68	34
Employment of particular classes or persons*	229	202	257	260	227	242	253	229	271	340	332
Other working arrangements, rules and discipline	457	436	535	618	640	735	833	1,078	1,106	936	689
Trade-Union status†	46	35	28	32	30	30	33	35	63	58	42
Sympathetic action‡	22	27	16	16	13	8	24	24	23	19	28
Other Causes §	7	15	13	4	—	—	—	—	—	—	—
Total	**1,426**	**1,339**	**1,719**	**1,714**	**1,746**	**1,989**	**2,419**	**2,648**	**2,859**	**2,629**	**2,093**

* Examples are demarcation disputes, disputes arising from the employment of certain officials, and claims for reinstatement of discharged or suspended employees.
† Trade-Union status includes refusal of trade-union members to work with non-unionists.
‡ In support of workers involved in stoppages at other establishments.
§ This separate classification was discontinued from 1953 onwards.

FIG. 26

indicates that matters for consultation have not provided fresh grounds for dispute. But consultation can on occasions be as bitter as negotiation.

The Bigger Buses Dispute of 1962 illustrated this. The management of London Transport were trying to improve efficiency. They wanted to replace existing buses by bigger ones, and to give bus operatives 40 per cent of the savings. They wanted to introduce, in some suburbs, single-deckers operated by one man. They wanted to experiment in Central London with 'standee' buses, half the vehicle with seats, and the other half with standing room only, and with a conductor remaining at the back. Finally they wanted to take advantage of the law permitting maximum speed to be raised from 30 m.p.h. to 40 m.p.h.

It was an attempt to alleviate the problem that afflicts almost all forms of transport, that is to say 'peak' and 'trough' periods. At the time, one-third of the whole fleet of 5,500 buses was used at peak periods (the so-called rush-hours, Mondays to Fridays), and not at all at off-peak periods. One-third of the fleet was idle for a large part of each week. The use of larger buses would remove the need for these peak-hours standby buses, and thus save fuel, maintenance, crews and capital expenditure. No busman would have been made redundant by the scheme since London Transport were at the time 10 per cent short of their needs for bus operatives. The scheme would have done something to alleviate that shortage.

It was not a pay dispute, nor was anyone going to lose his job. The busmen said that they were worried about their arduous hours of work, and also of the risks involved in operating standee buses, and in speeding up services. But responsible commentators agreed that it was basically a dispute over a plan to increase the efficiency of London's buses. Managements should not be too surprised to learn that the practice of consultation spreads the area of disagreement between employer and employed. This is part of the age-old experience of giving people freedom, and their abusing it. And this abuse is still a weak argument for restricting freedom.

So much of the transport industry in Britain is now nationalised, that it is tempting to regard the industry's industrial relations machinery as part of the idea of nationalisation. But many nationalised transport undertakings have, to a large extent, preserved the machinery they inherited from the former private companies.

For example, a National Joint Industrial Council was set up in 1919, for the Tramway Industry. It covered undertakings, both municipal and privately owned, concerned with operating trams or trolley-buses. It did not include motor-buses. Trade unions began pressing in 1934 for national negotiating machinery for operatives on privately owned motor-buses. They did not get it until 1940, and in the meantime the NJIC for Tramways changed into the NJIC for the Road Passenger Transport Industry, and covered all grades of manual workers, other than craftsmen, employed by municipal undertakings on tramways, trolley-buses and motor-omnibuses. At the time of writing craftsmen in private omnibus undertakings (National Council for the Omnibus Industry) were represented by a joint spokesman for the Amalgamated Engineering Union (AEU), Electrical Trades Union (ETU) and the National Union of Vehicle Builders (NUVB). Craftsmen in municipal undertakings were represented in a separate NJC for craftsmen employed in Municipal Passenger Transport Undertakings by the AEU, ETU, NUVB, the National Union of Sheet Metal Workers and Coppersmiths (NUSMWC), and the Amalgamated Society of Woodcutting Machinists (ASWM). In both cases operatives other than craftsmen were represented by the Transport and General Workers' Union (TGWU) and the National Union of General and Municipal Workers (NUGMW). The National Union of Railwaymen (NUR) have a place on the National Council for the Omnibus Industry.

We should note here the four different types of trade unions. Firstly, there are those unions that cover a single craft or group of crafts, like the AEU, ETU and NUSMWC, whose members work in a variety of industries, including the transport industry. These are known as craft unions. Secondly, there are those unions that cover a single industry or group of industries like the NUR and the Iron, Steel and Wood Barge Builders' and Helpers' Association. These are known as industrial unions. Thirdly, there are those unions representing semi-skilled and unskilled workers throughout a great variety of industries including the transport industry, like the TGWU, NUGMW, and the Clerical and Administrative Workers' Union (CAWU); these are known as general unions. Fourthly, there are unions that cover a single grade or group of grades of staff in a single industry or group of industries, including the transport industry, like the British Airline Pilots' Association (BALPA), the Transport Salaried Staffs' Association (TSSA) and the Associated Society of Locomotive Engineers and Firemen (ASLEF). These we may call special industrial unions.

The transport industry, like many others, has been afflicted by disputes among these four types of unions over questions of who should belong to which union. Thus, the NUR, regarded as an industrial union, has enrolled operatives who are entitled to belong to the special industrial TSSA or ASLEF. Moreover the NUR has been accused of poaching members from the craft unions, particularly the AEU and ETU, in railways workshops, where it has also clashed with the general unions, particularly the TGWU and NUGMW.

Negotiating machinery was first set up in the docks industry in 1920. The National Joint Council, although altered from time to time, lasted down to 1944 when its title was changed to the National Joint Council for the Port Transport Industry. The Watermen, Lightermen, Tugmen and Bargemen's Union as well as the general unions is represented on the Council. The National Dock Labour Board was set up in 1947 by statute to manage the labour force of the whole industry by a body representative of both sides of the industry.

The private sector of the air transport industry is also regulated by statute in its negotiating machinery. Section 15, s.s. (1), of the Civil Aviation Act 1949, says:

'The provisions of this section shall have effect for the purpose of securing that the terms and conditions of employment of persons employed by any independent undertaking constituted for the purpose of providing air transport services or of carrying out other forms of aerial work shall, except in so far as those terms and conditions—

(*a*) are regulated by or under any enactment other than this section; or
(*b*) are in accordance with an agreement for the time being in force between the undertaking and organisations representative of the persons employed; or
(*c*) are in accordance with any decision for the time being in force of a joint industrial council representing the under-

taking and organisations representative of the persons employed;

comply with the following requirement, that is to say, that they shall not be less favourable than the terms and conditions observed by the Airways Corporations in the case of persons engaged in comparable work, or, where the Airways Corporations do not observe the same terms and conditions for persons engaged in comparable work, are not less favourable than the terms and conditions observed for such persons by at least one of those Corporations.'

This is a case of the private sector of a transport industry being required by statute to fall into line with the nationalised sector in negotiating its wages and working conditions. The National Joint Council for Civil Air Transport has a place for private enterprise on the Employers' side. One of the difficulties in implementing this section of the Act is in the interpretation of 'comparable work'. By organising work in a different way from that of either nationalised Corporation the independents seem to escape the effects of the section.

The machinery for negotiating wages and working conditions, and for consultation, in the nationalised air corporations goes back to 1946. The agreements reached complied with the requirements of the Civil Aviation Act 1946.

The negotiating machinery of the nationalised British Road Services, from 1963 under the Holding Company, dates back to 1949, and complied with requirements of the Transport Act 1947. It is interesting to observe the names of the unions representing the three grades of workers covered by separate national joint negotiating committees: (*a*) Operating and other wages Grades—TGWU, Scottish Horse and Motormen's Association, United Road Transport Workers' Association of England: (*b*) Maintenance and Repair Grades—AEU, ETU, NUVB and TGWU: (*c*) Administrative, Professional, Technical, Supervisory and Clerical Grades—TSSA and TGWU.

In its general provisions as to terms and conditions of employment of Staff the Transport Act 1962, Section 72, s.s. (1), said:

'It shall be the duty of each Board, except so far as they are satisfied that adequate machinery exists for achieving the purpose of this sub-section, to seek consultation with any organisation appearing to the Board to be appropriate, with a view to the conclusion between the Board and that organisation of such agreements as appear to the parties to be desirable with respect to the establishment and maintenance of machinery for—

(*a*) the settlement by negotiation of terms and conditions of employment of persons employed by the Board, with provision for reference to arbitration in default of such settlement in such cases as may be determined by or under the agreements, and

(*b*) the promotion and encouragement of measures affecting the safety, health and welfare of persons employed by the Board and the discussion of other matters of mutual interest to the Board and such persons, including efficiency in the operation of the Board's services.'

The Act then made it necessary for Boards to notify the Minister of Transport and the Minister of Labour of any agreements made. It also permitted the Boards to join with other employers in establishing terms and conditions of employment of Staff. The Holding Company was brought within the provisions of the section.

The Transport Act 1962 was renewing provisions made by Section 95 of the Transport Act 1947. At the time of the passing of the 1947 Act some of the undertakings embodied in the Commission had already set up systems for negotiating wages and other working conditions. Some of these systems were so well established that it was decided to adapt them to changes resulting from nationalisation, rather than begin again with completely new systems. This applied particularly to the Railways and to London Transport, but in the case of some other undertakings it was necessary for them to consult with trade unions to create something quite new. For a number of reasons the Commission could not set up common machinery for all the grades and types of people it employed, unlike the airlines who have the one National Joint Council for Civil Air Transport.

In the railways, industrial relations have been formalised for a long time. Company representatives and trade unions, meeting in 1907, agreed to set up committees called 'conciliation boards' to deal with wages and hours of work for certain staff in the traffic grades. This step in formalising relations made such an impression on the railways that a wide range of operating and traffic grades are now referred to as 'conciliation staff'. They include drivers, guards, signalmen, station staff, permanent way men, goods and cartage staff and some of the railwaymen who work on ships, canals and docks. The Railways Act 1921 extended formalised industrial relations to salaried staff, including supervisory and clerical grades such as stationmasters, and booking clerks. This machinery lasted until the companies and unions agreed in 1935 to set up new 'Machinery of Negotiation for Railway Staff'. This was followed by another 'Machinery of Negotiation for Railway Staff 1956', and doubtless we shall see the machinery brought up to date, from time to time. Since 1950 the railways' machinery for negotiation has included joint consultation 'to provide regular opportunities for co-operation and discussion between management and staff on matters of mutual interest including working efficiency, use of manpower, and development of the industry'. Unfortunately this machinery was not able to prevent the bitterness that arose in 1962 as a consequence of Dr Beeching's proposals to turn the railways into an efficient, commercial undertaking. The one-day strike in October of that year was the first stern reminder that the unions had been keeping their powder dry despite the new opportunities for consultation. In fact, in that year one of the claims of the unions was that management had never really implemented this clause. This might have been partly due to the fact that the consultative machinery mentioned above applied to only one (i.e. salaried and 'conciliation' staffs) of the six main categories of British Railways Staff.

The other five categories were:

(1) railway shopmen, employed in shop maintenance and construction of locomotives, stations, tunnels, bridges, ferries, etc.
(2) workshop supervisors
(3) electricity generating and distributing staff
(4) professional and clerical staff
(5) officers and senior salaried staff.

The railway shopmen were those most affected by the 1962 Beeching proposals. There was machinery for negotiating with them dating from 1927, and this was embodied in the Railway Shopmen's National Council after nationalisation. Workshop

Supervisors have, in their Railway Workshop Supervisory Staff National Council, machinery that dates back to 1932. The Unions represented on this council are the TSSA, NUR, AEU, the Confederation of Shipbuilding and Engineering Unions, and the Association of Supervisory Staffs, Executives and Technicians. This last union is very active in the air transport industry in which the TSSA is not represented. The Electricity Generating and Distributing Staff have comparatively young machinery in the National Railway Electrical Council, formed in 1952. The Railway Professional and Technical Staff National Council is even younger: it was formed in 1958.

A significant development in negotiating machinery in the transport industry was that of the agreement in 1950 between what was then the Railway Executive, the British Transport Officers' Guild and the Transport Salaried Staffs' Association. This machinery was to cover staff earning salaries between £1,175 and about £2,500 per annum, grades we might expect to find beyond the scope of negotiating machinery.

The London Transport negotiating machinery for Clerical, Technical and Railway Operating and Maintenance Staff (other than Workshop Staff) goes back to the days when the undertakings were privately owned. Small changes were made when they were transferred to public ownership in 1934, and again following the transfer to the British Transport Commission in 1948. Other sections cover:

Workshop Staff
- (*a*) Wages Staff
  - (i) Underground railways
  - (ii) Passenger Road Services
- (*b*) Supervisory Staff

Electrical Generating and Distributing Staff
- (*a*) Wages Staff
- (*b*) Supervisory Staff

Road Passenger Services Operating and Maintenance Staff (other than Workshop Staff)
- (*a*) Wages Staff
- (*b*) Supervisory Staff

Control Staff

(*a*) Control Grades other than those employed in the Department of the Chief Electrical Engineer

(*b*) Control Grades employed in the Department of the Chief Electrical Engineer

Executive Staff

The forerunners of Inland Waterways Division of the BTC (now British Waterways Board) had negotiating machinery from 1943 and the NJC for the Inland Waterway Industry was established in 1948.

Seamen are mainly represented by the National Union of Seamen, and other unions interested in special grades are the Radio Officers' Union, the Merchant Navy and Airline Officers' Association, and the 400-strong Engineers' and Firemen's Union, Grimsby Steam Fishing Vessels. The protection of seamen from victimisation by employers has been the concern of the State for a long time. The first protective statute was the Mercantile Marine Act of 1850, but more important was the Mercantile Shipping Act of 1894. But most of the work done in improving the lot of seamen and officers has been achieved through the National Maritime Board, on which are represented employers and employees.

This, then, is a brief review of the industrial relations machinery for the major branches of the transport industry.

What are the special features of industrial relations in the transport industry generally?

(*a*) A considerable number of unions are interested in the industry (e.g. 17 different unions are represented on the NJC for Air Transport).

(*b*) Apart from the considerable number of unions interested in the transport industry all four major types are represented:
  (i) Craft unions (e.g. AEU, ETU)
  (ii) Industrial unions (e.g. NUR)
  (iii) General unions (e.g. TGWU, NUGMW)
  (iv) Special industrial unions (e.g. BALPA)

(*c*) Most of the industry is either nationalised or municipally owned. Much of the negotiating machinery is at present founded on statutory requirements or local government regulations. Much of the machinery had antecedents in privately owned transport undertakings so that it is well tried.

(*d*) Because the economic health of the whole nation depends upon efficient transport Trade Union leaders are able to involve the nation in the industry's disputes by threats and use of the strike weapon.

(*e*) Management in the industry is very 'vulnerable', in the sense that transport is a perishable commodity; any service lost by strikes is lost for ever. Other industries can stockpile and make up for lost time. Transport management cannot do either.

These characteristics call for certain responses by transport management. Firstly, transport undertakings must contain within their organisation, highly trained industrial relations experts, to match up to the demands of the negotiating and consultation machinery. Too often industrial relations branches have been the Cinderellas of organisation, and consequently have failed to attract men with the right endowments and dispositions. Secondly, all managers in a transport undertaking should study thoroughly the negotiating and consultation machinery attached to their undertaking, so that they may understand the opportunities it affords, and the limitations it imposes on managerial decision. Otherwise managers may tend to play safe all the time, to make absolutely sure that they do not fall foul of the machinery.

Thirdly, management in transport undertakings should devote considerable effort to the education of their employees to encourage a keen sense of duty, and an appreciation of their responsibilities to the community. There is no other protection against the vulnerability we have referred to. Negotiating machinery will not stop unions taking advantage of their strength and management's weakness. Only the disposition of workpeople themselves can prevent the bitter struggles that we have witnessed in recent years. On the other hand irreparable damage can be done by managements arousing suspicions that they are taking advantage of the sense of duty and public spirit of their employees.

SECTION III—GENERAL AND SPECIAL MANAGEMENT

CHAPTER XII

THE NATURE AND TASK OF GENERAL MANAGEMENT

In some transport undertakings the title 'general manager' is used to indicate rank, rather than the sort of management the bearer practises. For example, in some management structures the heads of main divisions below a managing director are called directors, and the directors' seconds-in-command are called general managers. Then we find managers reporting to general managers.

The term 'general management' as it is normally used in business means a particular sort of management. It means management that is different from special management. General and special are distinguished by the former having breadth, and the latter depth.

General management is defined by the three characteristics:

(*a*) its responsibility for more than one kind of specialisation in management,

(*b*) its duty to optimise the results of more than one kind of specialisation in management,

(*c*) its duty to judge an optimum position from special management claims.

Special management is defined by the two characteristics:

(*a*) its duty to maximise the result of one kind of specialisation in management, (*b*) its duty to advocate a maximised result from specialist management.

Management is specialised as follows:

(*a*) Finance (including Estates, Properties, etc.).
(*b*) Purchasing (including Contracts, Supplies, etc.).
(*c*) Production— (i) Passenger and freight control,
(ii) Vehicle control,
(iii) Maintenance control.
(*d*) Marketing (including Commercial, Publicity, Advertising, Selling, etc.).
(*e*) Personnel (including Establishment, Staff, Manpower, Industrial Relations, Welfare, Training and Education, etc.).
(*f*) Research and Development (including Forward Planning, Project and Development).

Here we are talking about *managerial specialisation* and not about organisational groupings of operatives (see Chapter IX), although managerial specialisation may be reflected in organisational groupings, and managerial specialisation may in its turn depend partly on organisation groupings.

We often overlook the fact that the stealthy growth of the division of mental, or managerial labour has produced much more dramatic results than the division of manual labour proclaimed by Adam Smith. Just as one workman used to do about eighteen distinct operations involved in the manufacture of a pin, so one business manager used to do all the distinct tasks involved in managing a business. He would find the money, and look after it: buy the equipment and raw materials: direct production: do the marketing: engage, dismiss, pay and otherwise attend to the needs of his workmen: and remain constantly on the look-out to improve his business. Now these various managerial tasks may be performed separately by men with titles like finance manager, purchasing manager, marketing manager, personnel manager and development manager.

These are the six fundamental aspects of business management. They rank as *first-line* managerial specialisations. As such they should be represented at a level immediately below a managing director.

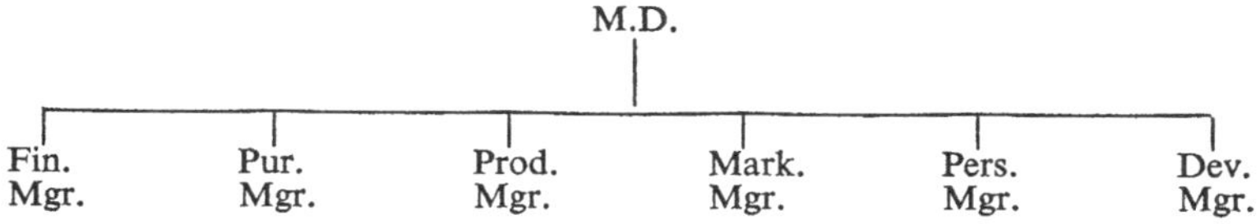

In this illustration each specialisation is represented by a separate *first-line special manager*, but this is not necessary. First-line specialisations can be successfully represented by second-line special managers, as long as a first-line general manager acknowledges responsibility for them. Thus:

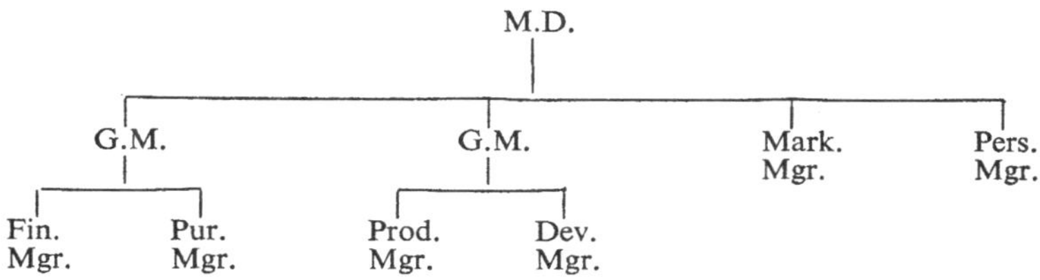

The effect of having first-line specialisations relegated to second-line special management may be to lower their status. General management control of just two specialisations would, however, make for strong co-ordination of the particular two.

If aspects of management not in the list given above are specialised and represented by first-line special management, then the business is unusual. This occurs mostly where businesses bring into organisation tasks that are normally carried out by contracting. For example, most businesses get their legal work done through private firms of solicitors, but some of them have their own legal divisions within the business organisation. Others include organisation and methods divisions instead of employing consultants, and so on.

The relative position of general and special management may be summarised as follows. Special management results from sharing the overall task of business management among a number of managers. General management is the means of reuniting the divisions made by specialisation. The pattern that results from use of general and special managers at various levels of authority is the 'management structure' of a business.

General management is always found at the summits of management structures; and additional general management may be found exercising authority over special management at lower levels. On the other hand, general management is often found in a subordinate position to special management. For example, in the management structure of the British Transport Commission in 1960, the position was as follows:

(*a*) For Divisions of the BTC (except British Railways and Road Passenger Services):

General Management
by
Commission

|

Special Management
by
Committees, Sub-Commissions
Advisers and Departments

|

General Management
by
Divisional Boards of Management

(*b*) In the case of British Railways:

General Management
by
Commission

|

Special Management
by
Committee, Sub-Commission
Advisers, Departments and
Central Staff

|

General Management
by
6 separate Area Boards

(*c*) And if we followed the railways organisation into regions (the organisation of each Area Board) we had the following picture:

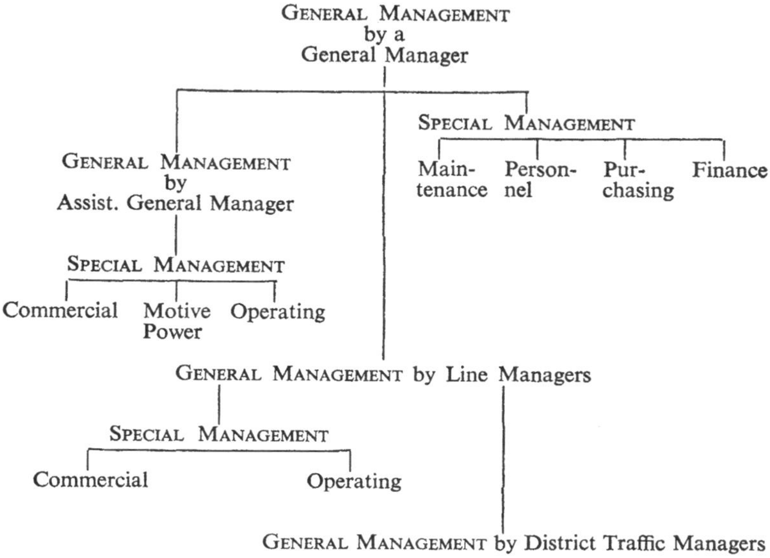

A general manager's relations with superior special managers are based upon the authority of the latter to establish standards that the former is required to follow in the exercise of his own authority. This arrangement makes for certain organisational difficulties. The partial authority of a number of special managers makes it appear that the general manager has a number of bosses. Sometimes we find awkward situations where general managers are subordinate to a *single* special manager, say the marketing manager. The relationship between general managers and subordinate special managers is based upon the authority of the former to grant or withhold resources requested by the latter. The dynamics of the relationship depend to a large extent upon the initiative of special managers.

General management exercises authority primarily to coordinate the activities of various subordinate special managers. Special management brings expertise that reduces error in the exercise of the authority of subordinate general management. General managers sometimes complain that the exercise of expertise, by superior special managers, undermines authority in organisation. On the other hand, special managers complain that the exercise of authority by general management deprives the organisation of essential expertise. One of the most important qualifications of a managing director is the ability to judge nicely the optimum position in general and special management relations.

The fewer the specialisations subordinated to a general manager, the stronger will be his powers of co-ordination. Conversely, the greater the number of specialisations subordinated to a general manager, the weaker will be his powers of co-ordination. We must not assume that strong powers of co-ordination are necessarily good for a business organisation, and that weak powers of co-ordination are bad. But in every business organisation, there are points beyond which co-ordination will be too weak, or in another direction too strong. Co-ordination may be considered too strong where one special manager is made to work in so closely with another that he is left no room for initiative.

A managing director may decide that the optimum position for his business is as follows:

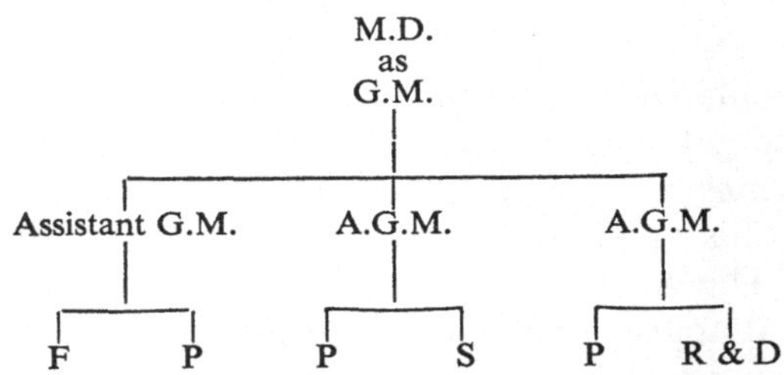

while another may decide that all he needs to co-ordinate closely are the purchasing and production tasks as follows:

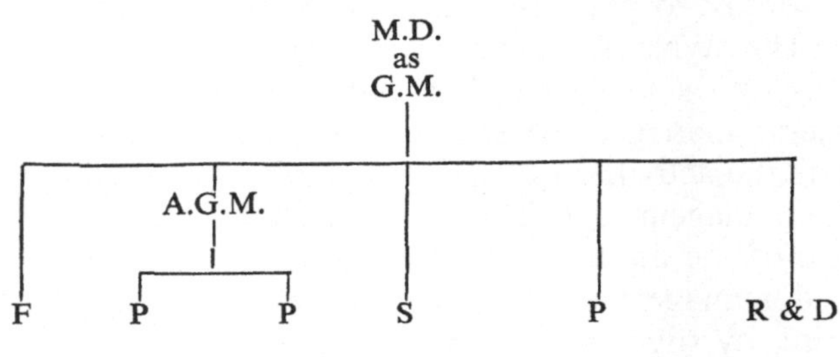

In the bus organisation illustrated in Chapter IX, the special management structure was described as follows:

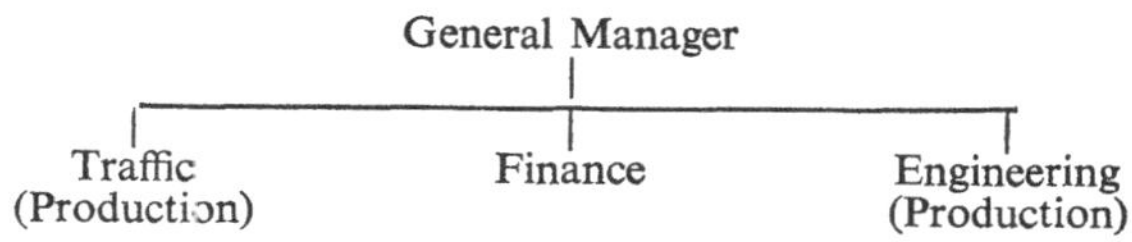

On the face of it the bus company decided to represent only two of the six first-line specialisations in first-line management, i.e. Production and Finance. Production was regarded as such an important specialisation that it was split into two; traffic production and engineering production, both represented by first-line management. On the other hand, purchasing, selling, personnel and development may not have been considered important enough for managerial specialisation.

This may be right for a bus company. Or it may be an illustration of general management concentrating excessively on production. We have evidence of transport undertakings buying unwisely, hardly bothering about selling, having bad management–staff relations, and not keeping up with modern trends. These shortcomings could result from a failure to specialise in these tasks.

It is not surprising that transport undertakings are sometimes preoccupied with production. Early struggles against mechanical and geographical controls were so great that they influence thinking to this day. But battles against sea and wind, against mountain and desert, against mechanical failure and shortage of power, have been largely won even though they continue. We have arrived at the stage where costs of production are important, where it is important to buy the right equipment, and where it is important to sell. Airlines lead the way in specialisation of the managerial tasks of marketing, personnel and development. But even they emphasise production by giving two or three separate divisions to it: passenger and freight control, vehicle control and maintenance control.

We might take the view that the bus company organisation chart illustrated an undeveloped form of management structure. It shows evidence of only the beginnings of specialisation in the various brainwork tasks of business.

On the other hand, transport undertakings that bring legal, medical and public relations functions into organisation, may be considered to have highly developed management structures. Specialisation in these secondary functions is, in fact, the hallmark of the big corporations in transport. Finally, we may find, on closer investigation, that the bus company organisation chart is misleading for someone trying to locate managerial specialisations. The manager in charge of the division labelled 'Finance' might, in fact, be a general manager, with two special managers reporting to him, one dealing with finance, and one with purchasing. The manager in charge of the division labelled Engineering may be co-ordinating specialisations in production and development.

CHAPTER XIII

FINANCE MANAGEMENT IN TRANSPORT UNDERTAKINGS

The normal tasks of finance management in business may be summarised as follows:

(*a*) borrowing money for the needs of the whole business,
(*b*) ensuring that investors' funds are not dissipated,
(*c*) keeping a situation that enables individual investors to withdraw funds,
(*d*) paying a fair price for the use of investors' money,
(*e*) ensuring that investors' money, and business revenue, is fed to the elements of organisation, in the right proportion and at the right time,
(*f*) seeing that money fed into organisation is not wasted, or used in an unauthorised manner,
(*g*) calculating profit, and in its distribution balancing the claims of the business, and its investors,
(*h*) preventing book values from diverging too far from market prices,
(*i*) choosing and using good accounting tools,
(*j*) controlling accounting, statistical and book-keeping staff.

Finance management in transport undertakings may be analysed in the same way, but the problems associated with the ten tasks, and the way they are carried out, are particular to the industry. Some of the peculiarities are not attributable to transport *per se*, but to the fact that the nature of the industry tends to encourage public ownership.

The fact that a very large part of British Transport is now either nationalised, or municipally owned, has an important bearing on the finance management of almost the entire industry. Public servants are now responsible for its finance management. Among their first acts was the buying out of private investors. Nationalised concerns even had to buy out municipal authorities. The finance management of most transport undertakings no longer has to account to private investors, but is 'publicly accountable'.

Most of the businesses that were launched with private funds must now regard the whole nation, or at least the inhabitants of a town, as the 'lenders' of the money invested in them. New borrowings must be made through someone like a Minister, with the approval of the Treasury, or through someone like a Town Clerk with the approval of a Town Council. The position of the four national Transport Boards was clearly indicated by the wording in the Transport Act 1962, saying that the Minister might, with the approval of the Treasury, lend to a Board any sums which the Board had power to borrow.

Parliament sets limits to managerial powers of borrowing as follows:

(*a*) Railways Board £1,100 million, and up to £1,400 million at the discretion of the Minister,
(*b*) London Board £200 million, and up to £270 million at the discretion of the Minister,
(*c*) Docks Board £120 million,
(*d*) British Waterways Board £30 million.

The British Transport Commission's interpretation of needs was not the deciding factor in how much money they obtained. The Government would lend as much as it could spare, having regard to other claims on the public purse. Management had to trim their plans to fit them to an imposed figure. The Commission pointed out that government cuts in planned borrowings for 1957 and 1959 amounted to £34 million, and that the Commission had to abandon re-equipment schemes already started, with serious capital loss.

The Ministry acted as bankers, and the Minister partly controlled the business by his power over borrowing. Some people said this was not efficient control, particularly as the Minister had no technically qualified staff to judge proposals for spending. The Commission argued that planning could never be long-term, because the Minister would never commit himself beyond three years. But what business can make up its mind on new schemes, certain in the knowledge that it can borrow money at a predetermined rate of interest? We may ask this of managements of profitable businesses, not running the risks of transport and public ownership. They are limited by the attitudes of investors. Willingness to lend is influenced by how much spare cash the lender has, and by the expected rate of return. The managerial task of borrowing is a task of persuasion, whose success depends partly on the skill with which the finance manager puts his case, and partly on the merit of the case he has to put. In the end it is the man who pays the piper who calls the tune.

The task of ensuring that investors' funds are not dissipated is imposed upon the managements of the Transport Boards by the 1962 Act which says,

'Each Board shall charge to revenue in every year all charges which are proper to be made to revenue, including, in particular, proper provision for the depreciation or renewal of assets and proper allocation to general reserve.'

As with any other businesses, what is bought cannot usually be sold for as much as was paid. Secondhand values are generally below new values for several reasons. Equipment begins to wear out. An improved design is in the offing, and so on. So money must be put aside to make up for the loss. A provision of this sort is called depreciation.

There is always a risk of equipment suddenly becoming valueless. It may be quite uneconomic to go on using equipment producing an inferior product, or with running costs that are high in comparison with new equipment. In this situation the old equipment is 'obsolescent'. It may be brand-new and in perfect working condition, and yet be obsolescent. The finance manager cannot fully protect investors against this risk. It has to be compensated for in payment for the use of money.

The BTC's method of providing for depreciation illustrates the problems associated with this particular task of finance management.

(i) They recorded a 'gross book value' for each asset, equal to its original cost (say £900).
(ii) They then estimated the useful life of the asset (say 10 years).

(iii) They then deducted from the net book value each year, equal annual amounts over the useful life of the asset (i.e. 1/10th of gross book value of £900 = £90 p.a.).

(iv) They then took this amount out of each year's revenue, and put it into a savings account, against the day when a replacement had to be made.

But it was soon discovered that this was not a sound method because cost of replacement is usually higher than original cost. For example, in 1958, the BTC set aside £25½ million calculated on the original costs of their assets, but the same calculations based on current costs would have produced a figure of £50 million. They were going to find themselves £24½ million short for the wear, tear and obsolescence for one year alone! The management of the BTC never had enough in the kitty to replace equipment. Re-equipment had to be financed by fresh borrowings; a situation that became more and more hopeless. By 1962 BOAC found they were sinking into the same position, and asked to be relieved of part of their capital burden.

In theory the long-term position of the BTC's nation-creditor was secure. If the nation invested £1,000 million in 1962, it could expect to see the money repaid in full by 2052 AD. In theory the nation-investor would withdraw a certain amount of money in each year of that period so there would be nothing left at the end. The amounts withdrawn by the nation-investor would be replaced by the Commission from revenue.

Capital investment was to be amortised (extinguished) by annual payments from revenue to a Capital Redemption Account. The Transport Act 1947 required the Commission to provide in ninety years an amount which, with accumulated compound interest at 3 per cent, would equal the total stock. This method was similar to that used by municipal authorities for financing their transport undertakings. By 1960 the Commission had credited their Redemption Account with £41 millions by annual doses of £4 million capital and interest. This repayment of borrowings might be regarded as notional, as the accumulated deficit on revenue account exceeded the total repayments.

Managers in private companies feel their responsibility to repay the people who have put money into their business. It is a personal responsibility. It is a case of not letting down people who have trusted you. Managers are usually conscious that investors are dependents of the business. But managers in publicly-owned undertakings lack this feeling of personal responsibility. Managers in transport have to sustain their sense of duty to 'investors', by integrity and training.

Looking after assets in the interests of investors involves paying attention to repair and maintenance. Transport undertakings are liable to face heavy, unforeseen maintenance bills over a short period. If failures occur through faulty design of a part, a fleet of vehicles may have to be brought in for modification. In order to even out good and bad years, some undertakings put money into a maintenance equalisation account in good years, and draw money out of it in bad years.

Management's duty to pay a fair price for money borrowed depends on the bargain struck with investors. With 'equity' capital, management must give investors their due share of the surplus of revenue over costs, if any. The problems in doing this are dealt with later.

The duty we will deal with now is that of paying fixed interest. Here management, to all intents and purposes, says to lenders, 'We will run our business in such a way that you can rely on being paid the agreed rate of interest on your money each year.' Some people criticise the financing of transport undertakings solely by fixed-interest-bearing stock. They argue that the method is psychologically bad for employees, whether they be managerial or operative. If a private business is financed wholly by equity capital, with no fixed rate of interest, all 'operating' surplus would be regarded as profits. Even if the business has only a small surplus, it has made a profit. But undertakings financed by fixed-interest-bearing stock have to deduct interest from operating surplus to calculate profit.

The profitability of a business does affect the morale of both management and men. But the real problem is that the operating surplus of most transport businesses is not large enough to attract equity capital. Some years before nationalisation the railway companies were not able to obtain equity capital, and were having to finance themselves by issuing debentures. So, while we may agree that equity financing is psychologically better, it is too much of a risk for investors in the present state of the industry. Borrowing capital at fixed rates of interest is not just a government imposition. Private investors would make just the same demand on the industry. The suggestion that nationalised transport undertakings should be allowed to borrow in the open market, with Treasury guarantees to back them is really asking to have one's cake and eat it.

The organisation of a transport business is like a human organism. If it is starved of sustenance it begins to run down. In a state of underfeeding, the organisation is prone to all sorts of ills. Sustenance in the case of business organisations is, of course, finance, and the metabolic process of business is the conversion of finance into the elements of organisation.

Operatives must be paid on time; equipment must be bought on time, repaired on time, refuelled on time, and so on. Organisation uses up cash continually. It is the job of the finance manager to see that cash is available in the right quantities when it is required. The Transport Act 1962 says:

'Each of the Boards shall so conduct their business as to secure that *their revenue is not less than sufficient* for making provision for the meeting of charges properly chargeable to revenue, taking one year with another.' (My italics.)

The transport undertakings must see to it that their organisations do not suffer by being starved of revenue. The 1962 Act made it easier for managements to fulfil this obligation by relieving them of restrictions in the Transport Tribunal's power over charges, and said, 'the Boards shall have power to demand, take and recover such charges for their services and facilities, and to make use of those services and facilities, subject to such terms and conditions, as they think fit'. The Act enabled managements to adopt a more businesslike attitude towards transport, and to moderate the rigorous concepts of public service. There was to be less emphasis on public duty and more emphasis on sound finance.

We must not, of course, make too much of legal permission for management to charge customers what they like. In the long run it is customers who decide whether or not to pay the charges the Boards levy. If they think the charges are too high, they will turn to an alternative such as private transport. Like all protected undertakings the Boards may decide only one of two things: either how much they will sell, or the price at which they will sell. If they decide how much, then they will have to sell at a price that will attract enough customers. If the Boards decide the price, then customers will decide how much will be taken up at that price.

The 1962 Act removed the characteristic burden of British transport undertakings. In future, 'none of the Boards shall be regarded as common carriers by rail or inland waterway'.

Transport organisations cannot be properly financed on a hand-to-mouth basis. The nature of the business is such that trouble can come quickly, and need a big cash outlay to overcome it. A disaster may occur, or a defect may call for modification to a great amount of equipment, and so on. It is important that management should create a reserve fund to finance exceptional demands. The 1962 Act makes each Transport Board 'establish and maintain a general reserve'.

Unforeseen 'vital' demands cause management's major difficulties in financial control. Unbudgeted claims for cash can be advanced in the interests of safety, or some other operational necessity. Control can soon be undermined if the finance manager is not alert enough to resist attempts by operational managers to evade it. Being a finance manager in a transport business calls for abnormal courage. There is always the risk that, if money is refused for something claimed to be essential, blame will fall heavily on the finance man if something serious does go wrong, even remotely attributable to insufficient funds.

Ernest Marples introduced in 1962 a new 'official' method of calculating the 'profits' of a transport undertaking. Accountants had told him that the proposed Victoria Tube Line would not make a profit. Revenue would cover operating costs, but nothing would be left to pay interest on £65 million of capital—and this would be £4 million a year, which is a big deficit for one short tube line.

So Marples asked an economist named Foster if the line could make a profit, in the sense that its *social benefits* could exceed *social costs*. Foster also had to consider incidental benefits and costs to the rest of the London Transport organisation.

Foster reported that *on these grounds* the proposed Victoria Tube Line would make a profit, and that this could be proved by:

(*a*) calculating social benefits in the same way as the social benefits of motorways were calculated, i.e. by putting a money value to estimated savings in journey times, (*b*) calculating incidental benefits to London Transport to include the fact that much of the cost of the new project was really the cost of making necessary modifications to existing equipment. For example, King's Cross, Warren Street and Oxford Circus Underground stations had already become overloaded, and would have had to be enlarged anyway.

It was argued that transport not only brings a service to passengers, but also to a wider community. It brings benefits not only to those who use it and pay for it, but to people who do not use it, and therefore pay nothing. Passengers pay for their travel, but nobody pays for relief of traffic congestion elsewhere, or the indirect trading benefits that follow improved transport. But why should not the people who benefit indirectly from the service pay the difference? Why should the nation subsidise the minority who would benefit from the Victoria Tube Line indirectly? The only answer to this seems that of expediency. It is impractical to identify the part of the community that benefits indirectly, and even more difficult to devise an equitable scale of charges.

If the Minister of Transport decides to run a service with unbusinesslike standards he runs the risk of unbusinesslike management. The distinction between the social service element and pure business must be clear. It is unfair to expect management to serve two masters; either it will develop the attitude of a social benefactor or strive for strictly commercial targets. In either case it will incur criticism. If government believes that transport should provide social advantage, whose beneficiaries cannot be made to pay, then government should pay. Business should then regard government payment for services as normal business revenue.

Book values of equipment can become unrealistic by being unrelated to market prices. The Select Committee on British Railways pointed out that the net book value of unremunerative branch lines, closed in 1958, averaged about £22,000 per mile. But the Committee said, 'this is part of the financial "archaeology" which is so much a feature of the railways' accounts'. An estimate of the realisable value of the lines was made in the Maintenance Equalisation Account, and for land and buildings it was taken as being in rural areas, £60 per mile in England and

£30 per mile in Scotland; but in urban and development areas the value was naturally higher and had to be assessed in each particular case. In some cases book values go *below* market price. But for its nationalised status there might have been a take-over bid for the BTC, whose book assets of £1,236 million, were estimated in 1960 as being worth not under £5,000 million. The 1947 Transport Act forbad the Commission to develop property except for their own use.

The Select Committee also criticised British Railways accounting procedures, when it said:

'Without an improved costing system and improved methods of ascertaining the profitability of Regions and services, management has been deprived at all levels of the assistance of two of its main instruments—financial results and costs. As a result, Area Boards have not known how efficient and profitable have been their various activities, and the full effect of their capital proposals cannot have been properly estimated by them, the Commission, or the Ministry. With modern methods and machinery, it seems to Your Committee unnecessary that decisions should have had to be taken by the imprecise methods that the Commission have employed. This seems to have been a serious shortcoming in management, the full effect of which it is impossible to gauge.'

Transport undertakings have particular problems in establishing costing systems. The more successful costing units are usually found in maintenance and construction workshops, similar to those in manufacturing industries. Here costing procedures can be integrated with accounting processes. The main difficulties come when trying to cost the other two aspects of production, that is to say, traffic and operations. Here costs are shared by several activities. Few pieces of equipment are used solely in one area, or on one route, or for one particular type of traffic. Even 'direct' or 'running costs' present difficulties that must be resolved by arbitrary decisions. It is even worse with 'indirect' or 'fixed' costs, whose apportionment is more often than not arbitrary. Basic approaches to the problems are similar to those of other businesses. Here is an illustration of a typical effort to analyse the costs of carrying goods, by railway, from A to B.

The service is first analysed in its four main parts:

1 Haulage
2 Wagon supply
3 Marshalling
4 Terminal Services

Then these four main parts may be subdivided as in the following two examples:

1 Haulage
 (*a*) long-haul (*b*) short-haul
 (i) cost of locomotive
 (ii) cost of locomotive crew
 (iii) cost of wagon crew (guards)

4 Terminal Services
 (*a*) wagon shunting
 (*b*) wagon loading and unloading
 (*c*) loading and unloading road vehicles
 (*d*) use of road vehicles
 (*e*) paper-work connected with traffic.

Good accounting tools, such as efficient costing, enable managers to be judged on factors that are within their control. For example, an airline should know if a short-fall in traffic to Germany was due to the number of Americans flying across the Atlantic being halved. Otherwise the airline might blame the wrong manager.

Now finally we come to the issue of the control of accounting, statistical and book-keeping staff. Chief Accountants tend to argue that accounting staff must be controlled by accountants, otherwise there is no check on their competence. General managers argue that they cannot accommodate a group of men who are not subject to their authority. There is something to be said for the arguments on both sides. Conflict is often avoided by gathering all accounting staff together under one roof where they can be controlled by accountants. Once this is done there are temptations to dispense with regional accounting. With new opportunities for division of accounting labour, organisation may be reshaped on accounting skills rather than regional needs. The whole business may be treated as one accounting unit in the interests of accounting efficiency, and not in the interests of general management.

CHAPTER XIV

PURCHASING MANAGEMENT

We often fail to appreciate the importance of buying. When we think about business our minds fly to production; that essential act of change. The way a business provides itself with equipment and raw materials is regarded as a secondary matter. Traders whose business involves no complex process of production are more likely to be aware of the importance of buying. The more technical becomes production, the more the purchasing process tends to be pushed into the background, until the consequences of its neglect, demonstrate that it is fundamental to production. Insufficient attention to purchasing is marked in most industries classified as service industries. Transport is no exception and has suffered from bad purchasing. It is tempting to believe that enthusiasm and the disposition to give a first-class service can overcome the handicap of poor equipment, whereas transport systems are bedevilled by equipment that nullifies the efforts of willing staff. Mistakes in the British tramp shipping industry began to have serious effects in the early 1960's. British Overseas Airways drew attention in 1962 to the effect of the purchasing policies imposed on them by Government. A decade after the creation of the British Transport Commission, breakdowns in services began to occur because of faulty equipment design.

In organisation, purchasing should have a place of equality with production. Purchasing is one way of doing business and production is the other. Purchasing is doing business by contracting: production is doing business by organisation. The role of purchasing management is complementary to that of production management.

Many businesses fail to give sufficient authority to purchasing management. They link purchasing and production by putting a purchasing section under a manager who regards himself as specialising in production management. The disadvantage of such an arrangement is that the voice of production dominates that of purchasing so that there is an inbuilt tendency to make rather than buy; to organise rather than contract.

The manufacturing firm's alternatives of making or buying, organising or contracting, can be exercised mainly on the maintenance side of transport undertakings. A transport business can buy engine-overhaul hours, or do the overhauls itself; or it can buy replacements for components, or strip them down and repair them in its own workshops. To some extent the alternatives apply to passenger and freight control. A carrier can get its traffic handling done by handling agents. Airlines often appoint handling agents in foreign airports. Shipping companies appoint shipping agents, loading brokers and so on.

The use of purchasing as an alternative to production is used comparatively little in vehicle control. Carriers do not often regularly use other companies' vehicles and crews. There are exceptions. Cyprus Airways has been an airline without any aircraft or crews. Many airlines have, of course, to charter vehicles and crews occasionally. Some shipping lines resort to chartering vessels when their own fleet cannot carry all the shipments demanded. But, in general, the 'operating' aspect of production is not a province for the purchasing manager. This we would expect, having regard to the nature of the business. The act of carriage is the most 'businesslike' of all the activities of a carrier. If the business ceases to carry, it becomes a travel agent, and is no longer a carrier. This still leaves management plenty of room for alternative strategies. It can strip the production process down to the essential act of carriage by buying in maintenance and traffic handling, or it can do as the railways have done in Britain, and become largely self-supporting in the three aspects of production.

Although purchasing is a fundamental managerial specialisation, the job of purchasing may be contracted out. As long as management continues to direct policy it may leave its execution to a contractor. Management cannot, without considerable risk, escape the brainwork of the function. The role of the ships' chandler is that of a middleman who has specialised in fitting out a ship for a voyage, with everything from pepper to block and tackle. Consultants brought in to work out detailed specifications in building offices, maintenance bases, shipyards, ports and so on, reinforce managerial specialisation. A complicated tangle of brokers and agents represent the buying activities of the Shipping Industry. Shipbrokers negotiate whole charters, and dispose of unwanted ships; shipping agents act as owners, general representatives in overseas ports; loading brokers procure ships for the traffic on offer. This elaborate network of contractual activity has enabled shipping lines to concentrate on production. Whether this is good or bad for the business is a matter for conjecture.

The relationship between purchasing and finance management is natural, bearing in mind the fact that finance is the raw material of a purchasing department. The finance manager ensures that there are funds available for the purchasing manager's needs. The purchasing manager gives as much notice as possible of his plans to buy, and consequent needs for finance. To re-lay a track, or buy new ships, many years' warning may be needed, so that the finance manager can raise fresh capital. Usually forward buying plans are insisted upon. The Treasury used to ask nationalised undertakings to make estimates three years ahead on a moving annual basis. The British Transport Commission thought that guarantees for three years ahead were inadequate. They thought that they should be guaranteed finance for buying five years ahead, as this was the minimum practicable planning period for big re-equipment schemes.

The purchasing manager should try to avoid sudden changes in delivery dates and consequential changes in the timing of payments. A fleet of vehicles delivered six months ahead of schedule can be a considerable embarrassment for a small business. So can a fleet that is six months behind schedule. The money will probably have been borrowed, and interest will have to be paid. The purchasing manager should not tie up in stocks more cash than is absolutely necessary. An engine spare bought a month before it is required is locking up money for a month. A spare wheel sitting on a shelf will be eating up pennies, if not shillings, in interest and rent. On the other hand, if the purchasing manager does not provide sufficient stocks to meet exceptional demands he may incur serious losses of revenue, because services have to be cancelled for lack of serviceable vehicles. A ship that is idle for a week or two because there are no propellor spares may lose a lot of goodwill. The purchasing manager has to tread the tightrope between wasting money, by buying ahead of needs, and losing money by buying after needs have arisen.

There must be a close relationship between purchasing and marketing management. It is obviously important in passenger transport, since purchases of equipment affect the enjoyment and comfort of passengers. Again we see a result of passengers being mixed up with production. A manufacturing firm does not usually have to ask itself whether a lathe, or a press, or some welding equipment has customer-appeal, since few of its customers will be concerned with them. Some firms, notably food manufacturers, encourage visits from customers, and these firms make sure their machinery is attractive in appearance. In transport the appearance of traction units, carriages, interior decor, and so on, is important. To purchase a ship without consulting the marketing manager would be unwise. However efficient a ship is in speed, reliability, safety and cost, if it does not 'appeal' to passengers it is a bad buy. And the same with aircraft, motor-coaches, railway trains and tramcars. This throws a responsibility on to the marketing manager to give warning—often early warning—of changes in fashion. On the other hand, purchasing management must give feed-backs to marketing management. If the former is going to buy 'attractive' equipment, the marketing people must be told as soon as possible, so that they can draw publicity from it. The purchasing side must provide marketable facts about its purchases. Marketing must supply purchasing with facts so that the latter can continually investigate sources of supply.

The development department of a transport business will have a say in drawing up specifications for equipment. In some cases purchasing management may have to restrain the production of specifications that are not commercially practicable. Just occasionally development people turn out ideas that cost a fortune to put into metal, or that no ordinary manufacturing could achieve. Purchasing people can often lead them gently to an acceptable compromise by familiarising them with the possible. One of the fruits of co-operation between purchasing and development may lie in the simplification and standardisation of equipment and spares.

A useful classification, of types of equipment purchased, for a transport business is as follows:

(*a*) main units (e.g. aircraft, ships, locomotives, lorries, plant and machinery),
(*b*) components (items that go to make up main units, e.g. engine parts, parts of transmission systems, etc.),
(*c*) consumable stores and bulk materials (e.g. fuel, lubricants, paint and construction materials).

This classification is not rigid. A power unit may be considered a main unit when thinking of the parts that go to make up a power unit; or it may be considered as a component when thinking of the parts that go to make up a vehicle. The classification draws attention to the interdependence of problems of maintaining supplies of main units and components.

Purchasing tasks may be classified as follows:

(*a*) planning a purchasing programme
(*b*) ordering equipment
(*c*) receiving equipment ordered
(*d*) storing equipment received

To this we might add a fifth task that usually falls to the purchasing manager because he is most qualified to do it, and that is disposing of unwanted assets.

Success in planning purchases for a transport business depends upon the ratios kept among main units and components. Failure to keep the right ratios may result in too much money being locked up in spares, or in a main unit being made useless for want of a relatively inexpensive part. There is usually a wide field within maintenance where planning is assisted by the fact that replacements arise regularly, and can be forecast within narrow time limits. For example, maintenance may be arranged so that every component in a main unit is given a 'life'. At the end of a predetermined period (say a thousand hours in service), each part has to be replaced, however good its condition is. Provided adequate records are kept, planning for this method of replacement is simple. Replacements that cause headaches are those that result from defects developing before the lives of parts expire. These give rise to unscheduled removals, in contrast to the former scheduled removals. Purchasing managers are able to limit the unexpected even here. Statistics show them the relations between defects and the frequency of traffic, or number of times vehicles stop, and so on.

Planning of purchases must take into account the logistics of production, i.e. the movement of supplies within organisation. Where equipment moves, as in a transport business, breakdowns may occur over a wide area. A solution is the placing of spares at every possible point, but this is a costly way of having spares in the right place and at the right time. It may be better to place all spares centrally and transport them swiftly to breakdowns. Or the optimum position may be modest stocks at certain places, and swift transport for the remainder.

Consumable stores like fuel and lubricants call for different policies. Probably the business will have to buy and stock fuel locally, as the only practicable alternative is to carry fuel on vehicles, which may be costly.

Important variables to be taken into account in planning are those of 'lead-times'. These are the periods between ordering and delivery. To establish realistic lead-times requires experience of suppliers. It is not always good business to demand absolute reliability from a supplier. It may be better to accept a compromise. Sometimes complete reliability can be obtained only at an uneconomic price. This is not submission to the inefficiency of suppliers; it is planning that allows some margin for less than absolute reliability, so that prices can be kept down. Last-minute orders demanding hasty rearrangement of a supplier's business are likely to be costly.

It is reasonable to take account of the unavoidable troubles that may afflict suppliers. Purchasing managers try to anticipate rises in the prices of their raw materials and equipment, or shortages or labour disputes. This calls for a careful, enquiring but sympathetic approach to relations with suppliers.

For most transport businesses, the critical purchase is that of vehicles. If the wrong vehicles are bought, they may create a lasting burden. For this reason, decisions to buy locomotives, ships, aircraft, or lorries is seldom left to a special purchasing manager; it is made by the managing director and the Board.

Not all vehicles present the same problems. At one extreme there are 'off-the-peg' vehicles, and at the other extreme 'tailor-made' vehicles. Between these two extremes there is a wide range of possible specification of individual needs.

The ocean-going tramp does a more or less simple and standardised job. The shipbuilder who specialises in building tramp vessels usually has a good knowledge of what they have to do. There are not a great number of variations in type of service. His customers are 'stock size'. If the shipbuilder is given size, speed and range required he can come up with a complete set of proposals, acceptable to the operator as a packaged deal.

But almost everything to do with a cargo liner has to be tailor-made. Beginning with such a fundamental and controversial question as to whether it should be powered as a motorship or oil-fired turbine-driven steamer. Then how much space can power-units be allowed to occupy; what shall be their weight, and that of the fuel they will require for maximum range; what can be allowed for crewing costs, maintenance costs, fuel consumption and so on? What shall be the size of the ship itself? Up to a certain point, the bigger ships are, the more efficient they are. The amount a ship can carry increases approximately with the *cube* of its dimensions. The resistance of a ship increases approximately with the *square* of its dimensions. So bigger ships need less power per unit of carrying space. This is data for a technical optimum. But technical optimum may not coincide with the optimum for estuarine and harbour channels the ship has to navigate. Or it may not coincide with the optimum for berthing facilities it is likely to encounter. Apart from the need to reconcile various operating optima, it is necessary to consider the commercial optimum for a ship. It is no good building a big ship that cannot be filled. A ship designed to achieve a cost-of-haulage optimum may be a white elephant from a revenue earning point of view. Purchasing management stands between cost-appeal and customer-appeal; between the production men and the marketing men. What is the good of buying equipment that is remarkably efficient, if the space it contains is unmarketable? Purchasing management should see that all views are made known when a business is considering buying vehicles.

There are usually more problems in buying cargo ships than in buying passenger ships. Human beings are fairly standard. By nature their needs do not vary widely. Cargo is of all shapes and sizes, requiring a wide variety of storage fittings and conditions. Purchasing management is often backed by drawing offices turning out specifications to the minutest detail. Even nuts and bolts may be specified in detail.

Although ships are a compromise, and aircraft are a compromise, and purchasing managers try to perfect these compromises, they must often observe statutory limits on the extent of compromise. The British Parliament has established principles of seaworthiness; it has fixed maximum permissible draught and the position of the official 'Plimsoll' mark. It has delegated legal responsibilities to Lloyd's Register of Shipping, which can circumscribe decisions of management. A ship is built and maintained along prescribed lines. In air transport specification for aircraft is done by the comparable Air Registration Board.

The process of 'receiving' equipment is often long and involved. The first stage may be the approval of prototype equipment, and the second may be an extensive trial period for production models, which the purchaser may watch carefully. These preliminaries may be hedged by the need to apply for a certificate of seaworthiness or airworthiness. Sometimes equipment is at first only half handed over, because a clause is built into the contract of sale permitting the vendor to maintain the equipment to his standards for a period. This enables the supplier to gain experience of the behaviour of his equipment under operating conditions. It is the duty of the purchasing manager to see the business is reasonably protected from the costs of defects developing within a short time of purchase.

There are the usual problems of storage of spares in a transport business. An optimum position must be reached, among such variables as economies of bulk purchases, cost of locking up money in stocks, possible revenue losses from inadequate stock, cost of physical storage, risk of manufacturers going out of business, transport costs and delays of centralised stores, increased costs of stock dispersal and so on.

There is a danger that the initiative in re-equipment will pass out of the hands of the carriers and into those of manufacturers. The early 1960's saw many airlines having to regard one- or two-year-old propeller aircraft as obsolescent, and having to buy jet aircraft. Carriers are not always as cautious as they were in 1962, when Saunders-Roe, Vickers-Armstrong and Denny hovercraft failed to secure a single order from operators, despite an intensive sales drive. The manufacturers were already spending several hundred thousand pounds a year on these craft.

Their commercial use was limited to short sea and river ferry for passengers; and low-density, high value cargo. But the sea ferry operator cannot make his business pay unless he has a long-life, low cost and reliable craft. The Denny sidewall craft was the only one that came near to these specifications. The quarter of a million pound Saunders-Roe hovercraft, powered by aircraft engines, and constructed of fine aluminium, travelled at a much higher speed than the 25 knots of the Denny sidewall. but no ferry operator, who had to use existing terminals, was interested in high speeds.

The test for cool nerves in airline management will come when manufacturers start pushing supersonic aircraft.

CHAPTER XV

PRODUCTION MANAGEMENT IN A TRANSPORT BUSINESS

Introduction

Sometimes a transport business uses a 'production-probe' to test the market. A limited service is run to an area to see whether it will attract any traffic. If the reaction is encouraging, then production is raised to a workable level. At this stage the service is one that would produce a profit, if it were reasonably well used. Providing transport to an area may cause the area to develop. An expanding economy may then give rise to increased demand for transport. Production is then stepped up to a second stage, to meet the demand it has itself created. Production anticipates demand to begin with, and demand eventually responds to production.

It is important to bear in mind that the *product* of transport is primarily 'arrival', and that 'carriage' is the *process* of production. Because passengers cannot be separated from the process, it becomes a secondary product. There can be considerable variations in processes and consequently in secondary products, to secure the same primary product.

Problems of process vary with geographical control on the system. The variables are geographical conditions and the extent to which the business has freed its equipment from their control.

One of the geographical controls on a tube railway is the rock through which it tunnels. London Underground systems avoided heavy handicaps by cutting tunnels through the 600-foot layer of London Blue Clay. Rotary diggers can cut through it at 500 feet a week. Geographical controls on road and rail are mainly topographical. In New Zealand road and rail are handicapped by mountains and fast-flowing rivers, but aircraft are free of these particular controls. Fertilisers can be brought to hill farms, and distributed by 'spraying' aircraft.

Geographical controls are not the only ones. Often a carrier's organisation is not a complete 'system'. It may have its own vehicles, but have to rely upon other organisations to provide terminals and track. Suppliers of terminals and track may then cause delays outside the control of the carrier. This is one of the most common risks in a carrier's business. Because customers are involved in production they constitute a control. In an attempt to persuade customers to co-operate in securing efficient production, British Road Services and Road Haulage Association used the slogan, 'Turn that lorry round!' as part of their contribution to the 1962–63 National Productivity Year. It was estimated that time wasted in this way added £100 million to the annual costs of the 200,000 vehicles in Britain's road haulage industry.

Production management in a transport business is different from that of manufacturing in one or two respects. Transport production stretches into the heart of a community. Once a network is established the community will never be the same again, and it will react to the change. Production processes in manufacturing are more manageable; they are more self-contained, farther removed from external pressures; isolable from other tasks of business. The roof and walls of a factory insulate production from avalanche, thunderstorm and fog. Temperature, humidity and lighting can be controlled within fine limits.

On the other hand production managers in manufacturing have not the same opportunity of creating goodwill by the nature of their processes. We are maintaining the distinction between process of production, and product. The production manager in manufacturing affects the goodwill of his business by the product itself.

It is important for management to appreciate the *optimum role* of their particular form of transport. Otherwise they may become involved in processes of production, for which their organisation is not well suited. Each form of transport has certain characteristics, that make it well able to do some things but not others.

Railways, characteristically, have high fixed or indirect costs. For one thing their tracks are expensive to construct and maintain. But if the track is well used, by well-filled trains, these costs can be spread over an enormous number of passengers and items of freight, so that the resulting cost for each unit can be relatively small. The conditions of carriage can be safe, regular and swift. But in the way that railways developed in Britain, production was not confined to routes on which tracks would be well used and trains well filled. Railways were producing transport for territories that enabled only bus companies to provide services in their optimum roles. It was once estimated that a railway would lose £5,000 a year, per mile of track, if in a year it carried no more than a quarter of a million passengers and carried no substantial volume of freight. But a bus company providing transport for the same number of people could make a profit of over £1,200 a year per mile of service.

The railways were not exploiting the selling points of regularity and speed, especially in the freight field. The railway system had grown from main arteries to smaller arteries, and from thence to a highly developed capillary system. The tiny channels for collection and delivery of freight reached into every small community; collection and distribution depots abounded: and the optimum production unit for these restricted channels became the goods *wagon*. Management had to think of production in terms of wagon-loads because they had developed a process of production that optimised the role of the wagon. So an intricate pattern of rumbling wagons, slowly moving from marshalling yard to marshalling yard, stamped itself on railways production. It needed draconian measures to about-face, and in accordance with railway characteristics think in terms of whole *train-loads* of freight moving non-stop and swiftly between major centres of population, that produce freight by the train-load. And it needed a management with the courage to cut away the capillary system and hand it over to road vehicles for which it afforded optimum conditions, and to go all out to take from these same road vehicles the bulk materials carried along distances that did not afford road vehicles optimum conditions.

We must remember that many railways all over the world have been developed on the system of 'production probes' mentioned earlier. Undoubtedly this system is responsible for creating numerous unbusinesslike routes, but it would not be just to blame the men who made the probes. They were often blazing trails across unknown territory, and were responsible for opening up vast rich tracts of land for mankind. We must also remember that railways often developed where there was no alternative road system, and road vehicles more suited to carrying small loads. Managements fall into error only when it becomes apparent that their particular forms of transport are not in optimum roles and they do nothing about it.

A practicable division of production management in a transport business, that is reflected in numerous organisations, is into the three aspects of (*a*) passenger and freight control, (*b*) vehicle control, and (*c*) maintenance control. These three may be broadly defined as follows:

(*a*) *Passenger and freight control*
Is imposed on the embarkation and disembarkation of passengers, and the loading and unloading of freight, from installations to vehicles, and vice versa; it may also be regarded as including the care of passengers and freight on-board vehicles.

(*b*) *Vehicle control*
Is imposed on the movement of vehicles from terminal to terminal, within predetermined tracks or courses.

(*c*) *Maintenance control*
Is imposed on the task of keeping terminals, vehicles and tracks in good working order, either by the prevention or speedy remedy of breakdowns.

The term 'traffic' is sometimes used to describe activities falling within the purview of passenger and freight control as defined above. But at other times 'traffic' is used to cover vehicle control as well, and at times to cover all aspects of production. The term has been avoided in this chapter to prevent confusion. The terms 'operating' and 'operations' are sometimes used to describe activities falling within the purview of vehicle control, as defined above. But at other times 'operating' and 'operations' are used to cover passenger and freight control as well, and at times to cover all aspects of the production task. These terms have been avoided in this chapter.

How is it possible to split up transport production in this way, and establish three separate controls? Usually there are, in fact, three separate aspects of production, *in the short run*. Thus, if vehicles have been scheduled for service, they move from terminal to terminal, whether there be few or many passengers. A 'scheduled service' is a guaranteed service that can be relied upon to run, irrespective of passengers and freight on offer. On the other hand, most of the movement of passengers and freight occurs outside vehicles. It is movement to and from, and therefore separate from vehicles. Finally, vehicles are usually maintained 'off-the-line', in order to avoid impeding production. Track and terminal maintenance can obviously be dealt with away from passengers, freight and vehicle movement. So it is clear that there is a reasonable basis for the separation of control over the passenger and freight, vehicle, and maintenance aspects of transport production.

Section I—Passenger and freight control

Figure 27 shows the major tasks that are involved in this aspect of transport production. Where different words are used, to describe the same thing for passengers and freight, these are shown in separate columns.

	Passenger and Freight terms	Passenger terms	Freight terms
1	Use of timetables		
2	Route determination		
3	Services extra to carriage		
4	Bookings on other carriers		
5		Reservations	Securing space
6		Tariffs	Rates
7		Tickets	Waybills
8	Load control		
9		Embarkation and disembarkation	Loading and unloading
10		Personal baggage handling	
11	Communications along routes		
12	Corrective procedures		

FIG. 27. *A list of tasks that may be regarded as coming within passenger and freight control*

All of these tasks require certain practical skills, and some of them additionally require social skills of a fairly high order. They should all be taught and seen in the light of the intention of this aspect of organisation, which is the care of customers and their property.

The company timetable is not just an operating plan, or a record of what was decided at a meeting in someone's office months ago. It is to enable the company to give customers quick and accurate information about when, how often, and what is the shortest time in which they can secure the 'arrival' they wish for, by using the company's services. The advice that a booking clerk gives a customer about the route he should take, will be given primarily in the interests of the customer. The customer may be interested in the shortest passage or scenic attractions, or he may be quite indifferent; in which case the booking clerk may be able to secure a commercial or technical advantage for his company.

Passenger and freight control should extend to quality of services, extra-to-carriage. A journey in a well-appointed vehicle can be spoilt by a cold cup of tea, or a dirty washbasin, or a rude remark from a steward or conductor. The attention of customers may need to be drawn to *en-route* services such as catering, secretarial services and so on.

Operatives in passenger and freight control should know about the services of carriers that connect with those of their own company. Customers get a poor impression if employees are interested in nothing beyond booking on their own services, and have no interest in the needs of the customer. The attitude of—'Well, we've done what you paid us to do, you're on your own from now on!'—is not good for business.

The job of reservations, or securing space, is not only to ensure that a place exists on a vehicle at the time of asking. The place must also be kept. The job of calculating the tariff or rate to be charged is seldom just a question of seeing that customer or company does not lose a few pence, a few shillings or even a few pounds. A wrong charge reflects on the efficiency of the whole operation. Sometimes an undercharge may involve the carrier in a heavy fine for the breach of international agreements on charges. The customer must be given a true record of the transaction between himself and the company, in the ticket or waybill which is his entitlement to carriage. Passenger and freight control includes the task of making sure that passengers are embarked, and goods loaded in such a way that passengers, cargo and vehicles are not endangered. For example, there are intricate problems connected with the loading and unloading of cargo of liners. A cargo liner may have scheduled calls to make at a dozen different ports, with consignments of cargo for each. To avoid damaging goods themselves, the heaviest items should be stowed at the bottom of holds, but the heaviest goods may be those required at the first port of call. Commodities likely to contaminate others must be kept apart. Cargo must be stowed in such a way that it does not upset the stability or trim of the ship, either transverse or longitudinal. The designer will have ensured that she is stable and that his weights are distributed so that the ship will float unloaded in an upright position and with the correct fore and aft trim to ensure adequate propeller immersion. Passenger and freight control should see that loading does not upset this balance. It is usual to prepare a plan, on some form of load or trim sheet.

Efficiency in embarkation and disembarkation is achieved by managerial care, and attention to detail. Systems have to be devised to check that customers are getting the service their ticket or waybill entitles them to; no more and no less. Certain documents may have to accompany passengers and freight; perhaps a passport, or a vaccination certificate, or a bill of lading. Passengers may have to be led, and goods carried, from assembly points to vehicles, and their 'loading' carried out in accordance with a plan prepared by 'load control'.

Loading and unloading passengers' personal baggage calls for careful control. Mistakes that seem trivial to operatives cause passengers inconvenience, and lose goodwill. The procedure may include giving passengers official receipts. Baggage has to be loaded on to the right vehicle without damage. This does not happen without planning when many dozens of vehicles, and thousands of pieces of baggage are around at all hours of the day. The loading of baggage will probably be included in the plan prepared by load control. It must take into account the destinations of individual passengers. Care must be taken with unloading, as with loading, to prevent damage. Finally, baggage may have to be delivered against a receipt.

Behind the scenes are the communications that keep stations ahead of traffic warned of its approach; not only of numbers, expected time of arrival and so on, but perhaps of the peculiarities of individual passengers or freight. Thus, operatives at destinations know what to expect and can prepare for customers' arrivals.

This aspect of transport production includes a whole range of vital procedures connected with the explanation, settlement and perhaps correction of service failures. Passengers may have embarked on the wrong vehicle, and disembarked at the wrong place; a technical fault to vehicle or track may cause a suspension or cancellation of service; the weather may cause delays to services; luggage may be lost; cargo may have to be jettisoned to save a ship; an accident may occur that damages the persons and properties of customers. Passenger and freight control has to foresee all these eventualities and prepare certain routines to ensure that the best is made of a bad job.

This branch of management is concerned with customers and their belongings. In their relations with other managerial specialists they should represent the point of view of the customer.

Collecting payment for goods sold is normally part of marketing. Payment is usually made 'in the market'; it is not usually made to someone on the factory or workshop floor. For one thing, production may take place a long time before the product is sold; production anticipates marketing. But in transport marketing anticipates production; the selling has been done before the customer comes along to pay for his ticket, or for the charges for shipping his freight. Not always, but usually, the customer of a transport business pays when he comes along to play his part in the production process, and he pays it to an operative who is primarily concerned with production and not marketing. Finance management, therefore, has to devise procedures to prevent loss through the fraud or carelessness of operatives in passenger and freight control.

The link between passenger and freight control and purchasing is closest on questions of terminal equipment, and vehicle fitments. The links between passenger and freight control and the managements of other aspects of production are, as we would expect, very close. The safety and comfort of passengers that is the concern of passenger and freight control, depends very much on the work of vehicle control and maintenance control. None of them can work efficiently unless there is a continual flow of information among them about each others' actions. The link between passenger and freight control and marketing is strengthened by the fact that much of what is done by passenger and freight control is of commercial significance. If passenger and freight control approach their task as if it were a purely technical production task, calling for no social skills, they will soon upset customers. It may be very 'efficient' to spend the minimum of time on personal problems of passengers and shippers, and to treat each as a unit to be processed as speedily as possible, but it may be adding to the difficulties of marketing. The way that control is exercised over the movement of passengers and freight can increase or decrease the goodwill enjoyed by the business, and the work of the marketing people is very much influenced by that goodwill.

Having emphasised the need for care and attention to passengers and freight, we should note the need for control in the interests of organisation. Control should be exercised to ensure an orderly flow of passengers and freight. Arrangements must be made to verify customers' entitlements to carriage, and to prevent their conduct from impeding production.

Section II—Vehicle control

The main tasks falling within vehicle control are:

(*a*) using vehicles
(*b*) using route equipment
(*c*) using terminal equipment
(*d*) using communications equipment.

Control over the use of vehicles is largely a matter of controlling standards of training and performance of vehicle crews. Managerial control is usually supported here by some form of state licensing system, imposing certain standards of training. Beyond this, management lays down normal procedures, setting limits to the use of vehicles (e.g. rate of acceleration, cruising speed, maximum speed, overall weight, stopping distances, permissible weather conditions, etc.). Managements generally regard statutory limits on vehicles as minimum standards, and tend to pitch their own standards somewhat higher. As well as spelling out normal procedures for vehicle use, managements may also specify emergency procedures, particularly where it is necessary to train for action in emergencies.

Inspectors are used to report on standards of training and performance of operatives, but there are other means of 'keeping an eye' on what happens on flight deck, or bridge. Logs and voyage reports are useful sources of information.

Managerial control on the movement of vehicles that are 'rolling' is partly through standing orders, recorded in navigational or journey plans, and partly through control signals given to vehicle commanders *en route*. Signposts, or navigational aids, are part of managerial control, and a good deal of attention is given to planning their provision. Stop-go visual and audio signals, and other more sophisticated communications, afford more control. Thus, a ship's captain can be ordered to change course and call at a port not included in his itinerary, by instructions over radio-telephone.

The establishment of a route and its equipping is in itself a measure of control. Stopping-places form the main outline of routes, but it is often advantageous to specify the course to be taken between stopping-places. Various forms of directional signs promote the ends of keeping vehicles within track and performance limits. Managerial control of moving vehicles is exercised primarily in the interests of safety; and particularly to avoid collisions between vehicles by keeping them safe distances apart.

In the use of terminal equipment, management control stopping and starting techniques, approaches and departures, to prevent vehicles damaging equipment, and equipment damaging vehicles. The positioning of vehicles is planned, and terminal facilities for refuelling, lubricating, watering, catering, and so on are provided. Terminal equipment includes important communications devices.

While vehicle control is exercised primarily to achieve safety, it is not right to take the attitude that safety is the only thing that matters. After a certain point safety measures, like any other sort of effort, give diminishing returns. As expenditure mounts up, more and more money is required to achieve less and less additional safety. If a customer entrusts his person or belongings to a transport business, it is not reasonable for him to expect there to be absolutely no risk. He faces the fact that service is provided as a business, and business standards cannot be perfect. They are what business can provide at the price customers can afford to pay. Vehicle control has to be exercised with constant regard to cost, and to revenue.

Critical purchases from the point of view of vehicle control are those of fuel, lubricants, crew subsistence and so on. This calls for co-operation with purchasing in planning. Decisions should be notified quickly to passenger and freight control, and maintenance if these latter two have to modify their own plans.

Finally, vehicle control is vitally important to marketing in its task of securing operational reliability.

Section III—Maintenance control

A strategic decision in maintenance control is that establishing the point at which something will be done to keep equipment in running order. There are three alternatives:

(*a*) replacing components regularly, so that parts do not fail through age,
(*b*) replacing components when signs of impending failure appear,
(*c*) replacing components when failure occurs.

In the first of these alternatives, management estimates the 'life' of each component. A life is notionally ended well before it might reasonably be expected to fail through age. Thus, we might expect a certain bolt to last five hundred hours before it needs replacing, and give it a notional life of four hundred hours to almost eliminate the risk of the part failing through being worn out. The advantages of the policy are that withdrawals of equipment can be planned to give an even flow of maintenance work, and to minimise disruption of service. The number of unexpected withdrawals is minimised. The main disadvantage is the waste from building-in safety margins into 'life' estimates. Cautious preliminary estimates are revised in the light of experience, so that wasteful margins are reduced. Another inherent disadvantage of the system is that disturbance of an assembly of components may produce faults. This is reflected in the opinion that while something is running well, do not touch it.

The advantage of the second system is that the waste of component 'life' is reduced, without waiting for a breakdown. The signs of developing defects should give enough warning to enable the main unit to get back to base. The main disadvantages are the amount of training or experience that operatives need to discern signs of impending failure, and that on occasion signs will not give enough warning, so that equipment may be out of action at awkward times and in awkward places.

The advantage of the third system is that main units are not interfered with, until it is absolutely necessary to do so. The life of each component is as long as it can possibly be. The disadvantages are that maintenance programmes may be erratic, and breakdowns may disrupt services.

The second major policy area in maintenance control is concerned with the alternatives of replacing components from contractors, or from the firm's own workshops. Shall it be replacement by newly-constructed or reconstructed parts? Allied to the question of component replacement is that of main unit replacement. Shall the assembly of main units be carried out by contractors or in the transport company's own organisation? Most of the main unit construction jobs, for example, ships, aircraft and road vehicles, are today tasks of assembling components manufactured by thousands of small specialist firms. Whole vehicle construction is expressly forbidden by statute for some of the nationalised transport undertakings, but the railways have a long tradition of extensive main unit construction.

A certain amount of running repair will probably have to be carried out away from the main maintenance base. Maintenance control must keep the right balance in dispersal of resources. It has been possible for shipping lines to change their maintenance policies in recent years, and to send propellers by air to arrive within a day or two of despatch. Maintenance control is exercised to reconcile the optima of minimum costs, and minimum delay and consequent minimum loss of revenue.

In air transport, maintenance is controlled partly by fail-safe systems. These provide standby parts to take over the work of service parts, immediately the latter begin to fail. Sometimes an automatic process has an alternative manual process; for example, if a hydraulic undercarriage fails, the undercarriage may be lowered by hand.

Problems of track maintenance vary from one form of transport to another. Railways are self-contained, usually owning their tracks and able to strictly control them. Railways track maintenance is controlled to fit in with the work of the other two aspects of production. On the other hand, if a landslide or a collision blocks a railway line, despite all the opportunities for planning, services will probably be dislocated. The nature of railway tracks is restrictive and offers few alternative routes. A road haulier has little control over track maintenance, but if a road is blocked he usually has at least one alternative. The condition of air and sea tracks often cannot be controlled in the face of natural elements, although there are limited possibilities, for example, with ice-breakers. Bad meteorological conditions are often widespread and difficult to escape from by change of course. It is possible to avoid local thunderstorms and to keep out of the path of whirlwinds, which are less restrictive than widespread fog or ice.

Efficient maintenance control depends upon adequate communications. Information about breakdowns, notification of service delays affecting maintenance schedules, notification of the position of stocks of spares; these and many other aspects call for quick and reliable communication.

Finance management has to maintain reserves to meet 'crash' programmes. Some organisations have accounting devices to even out expenditure, from one year to another. Money is paid into maintenance equalisation accounts in good years, and drawn out in bad years. Because maintenance control depends so much on purchasing there is a tendency for maintenance and purchasing to be closely co-ordinated. Thus, a chief engineer may co-ordinate a maintenance engineer and a purchasing manager.

Close co-operation of maintenance control with passenger and freight control, and vehicle control, is essential. An aim of maintenance control is to avoid preventing the other two from earning revenue. Maintenance control has a similar responsibility to marketing management. There are more marketable and less marketable times. It is more difficult to sell bus seats at midnight than it is at midday in most places. For the sake of economy, maintenance should be confined as far as possible to less marketable periods of time.

Motive Power Control

In sea and rail transport, and to some extent air transport. another aspect of production management has to be added, Where power production calls for considerable skill and effort, its control is generally exercised by separate organisation. In shipping, distinctions are blurred by power production requiring organisation on the vessel, subject to vessel control. But the distinction is usually reflected in land establishments.

In rail transport, power production can be separated to a greater extent. Getting up steam is a job for depot people, and drivers can take over with stores of power to hand. With electricity we have a system of power distribution that is separate from vehicles, and more closely allied to track control than to vehicle control. Also, of course, electrical engineering is highly specialised, and this tends to encourage separate organisation.

While over-production is a feature of modern industries, producing in anticipation of demand, we seem to hear more about it in transport. We might well conclude that the situation is endemic; and that the cause lies in unbusinesslike approaches. In most industries over-production is curbed by the continual process of high-cost producers going to the wall. Low-cost firms reduce prices, and keep them reduced long enough to drive high-cost firms out of business. But in some forms of transport—for example, sea and air—operators have renounced the right to behave in this competitive way. Price warfare, it is sometimes claimed, is inherently dangerous.

There are usually frills that can be cut to reduce costs, before the efficient firm begins to affect safety. Also there are effective ways of ensuring safety other than by making price agreements. Price agreements among shipowners in the nineteenth century did not remove the need for Parliament to establish the Plimsoll Line.

Part of the trouble is that communities resist the curtailing of transport services. They tend to regard transport as a 'public utility'; in the way they regard water, electricity, street lighting and so on; something that must always be on tap. This is why so many undertakings become municipally owned. Publicly-owned transport businesses make losses, and people look on them as necessary burdens, unless the losses become scandalously high! The position is justified by arguments that transport brings indirect and often hidden benefits to a community.

The attitudes of management also contribute to over-production. Managements are afflicted by a temptation to cure 'over-production' by 'more production'. They may argue that they are not doing well because they are not giving a good service. Services are not frequent enough to satisfy customers. Competitors can be beaten only by stepping up frequencies and giving a better service! This sounds plausible, but it is not a businesslike argument; it is an argument dominated by the thinking of production management.

Commercial reasoning would be that seats may be 'filled' either by attracting more passengers with reduced fares, or advertising. Otherwise the number of seats on offer should be reduced.

There are many 'production' arguments against this line of thinking. One is that if a transport business reduces services, it becomes less well known. A transport system is its own advertisement; a big system is a big advertisement and a small system a small advertisement. This is true as far as it goes, but it does not acknowledge the alternative of advertising by press and poster. An optimum position may well be achieved by a small cutback on production, the use of the consequent savings on conventional advertising, and a resulting increase of passengers to fill the reduced services. A well-advertised once-a-day service may be more remunerative than poorly-advertised twice-a-day services. General management has to recognise and resist production management's tendency to regard extra service as the only way of competing with rivals.

Mention must be made of the difficulties facing production management in a transport business, in establishing yardsticks with which to measure production. Mance in *International Sea Transport* illustrated managements' difficulties in a paragraph on tonnage measurement: 'The gross tonnage of a ship is the sum in cubic feet of all the various enclosed spaces of a vessel divided by 100. The net tonnage is the gross tonnage less certain deductions on account of crew spaces, engine-room, water-ballast and other spaces not used for passengers or cargo. The deadweight tonnage or carrying capacity is the number of tons (of 2,240 lb) of cargo, passengers, fuel and stores that a vessel is capable of carrying when charged to the load line. Displacement tonnage is the weight of the vessel and contents in tons when charged to the load line in sea-water. It is evident that gross tonnage is always greater than net tonnage. As a general rule for merchant vessels of ordinary type the deadweight carrying capacity is always greater than the net tonnage and is usually greater than the gross tonnage. As an example, a cargo steamer with a nominal deadweight tonnage of about 8,000 tons of cargo, fuel and stores will have a displacement of about 11,500 tons, a gross tonnage of about 5,200 and a net tonnage of about

3,200. In principle, harbour and canal dues have been levied on the net tonnage of vessels, which is supposed to represent the earning capacity of the ship.'

Different ways of measuring capacity and load afford plenty of room for misunderstanding. There is no single measure in any form of transport that will serve management in its approach to all the problems of production control.

CHAPTER XVI

MARKETING MANAGEMENT

Marketing's widest meaning is expressed in the simple mechanics of trading.

1. Sellers consider available markets.
2. They take wares to a market-place considered convenient for buyers.
3. Buyers consider available markets.
4. They go to convenient market-places.
5. Sellers make displays to draw the attention of buyers.
6. Buyers examine the displays.
7. They consider price.
8. They decide to buy or not to buy.
9. If they decide to buy they hand over money.
10. Sellers hand over goods, or services.

However involved is talk about marketing, basically it cannot depart from these simple truths. The jargon of market-research, supply and demand, buyers' psychology, advertising, sales promotion and distribution should not be allowed to obscure the facts.

There are two main characteristics of traditional marketing worth noting because they throw light on the problems of marketing transport. Firstly, there is a physical 'market-place'; a no-man's-land for buyer and seller: common ground specialised to the exchange of money for goods. Secondly, there are opportunities for *single-encounter* transactions.

Not all marketing is conducted along traditional lines. Transactions do not always take place in a physical market. There may be no half-way house, no neutral meeting place for producers and consumers, for sellers and buyers. Producers may deliver directly from sites of production to consumers' homes. Or consumers may go to sites of production, collect goods and carry them away themselves. Where consumers buy services they often have to go to sites of production, for example, to the stopping place of transport companies.

If there is no market-place there is less chance of convenience for both parties. Either the convenience of customers will adversely affect the location of production; or the convenience of production will adversely affect the length of journeys for buyers.

In the transport industry customers have to come and collect 'services'. There are inevitable problems of reconciling the convenience of customers, and the convenience of production. Part of the marketing management task is concerned with where customers 'collect' services. Probably a greater rather than a smaller number of collecting points would be wanted so that every customer has a nearby collecting point. A person living in a Wiltshire village, and wanting to arrive in Edinburgh, would probably prefer to board a train in his village and step off the same train in Edinburgh, rather than travel to London and pick up a main line train from there. The same applies to farmers shipping cattle. Farmers would prefer nearby railway collecting points. There were, in fact, over 2,000 such collecting points for cattle in Britain in 1961, but it was planned to reduce these to less than 200 in 1963. Sometimes an easy marketing situation makes the production position difficult.

A transport system optimising the role of a trunk line carrier, from the point of view of production, should locate collecting points in highly populated areas. Railways optimise their role by being mass producers of transport. No other form of surface transport can match their ability to carry traffic with safety and speed at great volume and density. Railways can characteristically discipline mass movement, by their signalling and operating procedures, and the support of legal regulations. And the mass movement is economic because small crews can move great loads. All the advantages of this pattern of production can easily be dissipated by a marketing policy not based on a clear assessment of the best interests of customers. The best service railways can give their customers is this fast bulk travel, not the convenience of thousands of collecting points.

The classical marketing situation that obtains in a physical market-place enables production to be freed, to some extent, from control on its location exercised by the 'convenience of the customer'. Transport, inherently, has not got complete freedom to locate production where it most suits the techniques and economics of processes of production. The best that can be done for production is to establish a reasonable compromise between its needs and those of marketing. But we must always bear in mind that production needs and marketing needs come together at terminal points in transport systems.

The classical marketing situation also makes 'single-encounter' marketing possible. A first-time buyer goes *to the market-place*—not to the individual seller—believing that he is likely to find someone there, selling what he wants to buy. The market-place is what initially draws him toward the seller. The buyer knows that once he is in the market the seller will attract his attention to his wares. In general, where marketing is not conducted in a market-place, the buyer has to be attracted all the way to the individual seller. This, in a sense, causes there to be more than a single-encounter. In market-place buying, the buyer need not have addressed the seller before the former arrives in the market. The buyer can do his buying, and not concern himself with the seller again, unless he has fresh cause. But if the seller has to attract a buyer he must 'encounter' him before he sets out to buy. This encounter may be through advertising or by personal meeting. But anyway there are two encounters that may go wrong, and have to be watched as part of the marketing process.

Another way in which transport marketing differs from classical marketing is this. The producer of transport often has difficulty in displaying his actual wares to first-time buyers. This is not so in the case of the second-time buyer, who has experienced the product as a consumer. The potential buyer of transport has not the opportunities of examining the product, as has a potential buyer of vacuum cleaners. Transport marketing has to resort to notional representation of the product. The display is an idea; not the product itself. With a variable mixture like transport involving process of production (by way of carriage) and product (by way of arrival), it is difficult to fashion a comprehensive notional representation. Does one show pictures of sunny beaches on arrival, or the conditions of travel *en route*?

In advertising the marketing manager must allow that the product is arrival. So his display, logically, should include

FIG. 28. *Example of BEA poster*

FIG. 29 *Example of British Railways poster*

destination. So he may advertise the Changing of the Guard in London, or the Notre Dame in Paris, or the Empire State Building in New York: he advertises places. But this may help competing forms of transport, serving these cities. So, built into the picture of a place, there must be a crystal-clear message to travel by a certain carrier. The marketing manager cannot avoid advertising the production process, but as this is not the primary product it must take second place, and yet at the same time be strikingly effective. This calls for considerable advertising skill.

However well the job is done, notional representation of a product provides greater room for misunderstanding, and consequent dissatisfaction, than does the display of actual products. Apart from careless, or misleading advertising, the customer may imagine he is buying something different from what he gets. For this reason marketing management should keep a careful eye on customer complaints about having been misled.

There is another problem. Where shall the notional display of wares take place? Shall the ideas be displayed at the point of production? The railways seem to believe they should. Or should the displays be near or in the homes of consumers? Airlines and shipping lines get into the homes through newspapers; railways are beginning to do so. Few transport undertakings were using television at the time of writing. They probably felt they could not afford to, but one might argue that they could not afford not to. Should the display be in customers' places of leisure, such as clubs, hotels, and so on? Once again airlines think so; but then, of all transport undertakings, they have the most aggressive advertising policies.

Although transport is usually produced in anticipation of demand paradoxically it may sometimes be 'ordered'. It may be ordered ahead of production, as when seat reservations are made, or space is secured for cargo. The significance of this is that it gives rise to yet another market encounter.

Finally, the mechanics of marketing may be complicated by the fact that money is not always paid over immediately in exchange for goods or services. Goods may be handed over on credit, as in the case of a television set that is obtained by a small deposit. Or money may be paid over in exchange for an entitlement to service, as in the case of a theatre ticket. With the introduction of credit travel, especially by airlines, the transport industry now experiences both complications. By paying money on a separate occasion the customer engages in another marketing encounter. So this may well add up to at least four marketing encounters: the first at the advertising or display stage; the second in selling an entitlement to travel; the third in reserving a place; the fourth in delivering the product by act of carriage. This helps to explain the extensive marketing interest in transport operations.

So far we have taken a mechanical view of marketing—revolving around facts like the market-place, nature of wares and the behaviour of buyers and sellers. Clearly these are the marketing facts that affect the organisation of a transport business. We must turn now to the economic viewpoint to discern those facts about marketing that have a direct bearing on the prosperity of a business. Here it is not so much a matter of the way in which marketing is done, but the effect that marketing has. From a mechanical viewpoint a market consists of people and things. From an economic viewpoint a market *per se* does not consist of anything. A market is *a range of quantities* that will be bought under differing circumstances. These vary with the forces of supply and demand, and result in the buying of small or large quantities. Thus the amount of travel that will be bought depends firstly on how much is available to be bought, as carriers set an upper limit by the amount they put on the market, and secondly on people's views of the price asked for it. Each person will weigh up to a lesser or greater extent whether or not a carrier is giving value for money. A person who travels has, in effect, decided that the travel is worth more to him than the money he paid for it. People's views on the worth of travel *at a certain price*, is what the advertising people work upon, in the hope of bringing about favourable changes of views. People can be persuaded to change their minds from thinking that a particular arrival is not worth £1, to thinking it is worth £1. For example, their attention may be drawn to a hitherto unconsidered aspect of beauty at the destination. On the other hand, the carrier has views on worth that are largely shaped by his costs. He will be very reluctant to go on for any length of time supplying transport at a price that does not cover his costs of production.

From the economic point of view the optimum marketing policy is not necessarily that which results in the sale of the maximum amount of transport that a business can produce, even where, right up to the maximum, transport can be supplied at a cost which is below selling price. The following table illustrates the position of a business whose costs of production are rising.

Passenger miles produced	Cost price d per mile	Selling price d per mile	Total profit
500	4	12	4,000
1,000	4	11	7,000
1,500	5	10	7,500
2,000	5	9	8,000
2,500	6	8	5,000
3,000	6	7	3,000

FIG. 30

This shows the danger of over-simplifying the problem of fashioning a marketing policy. Enthusiastic selling is not a panacea. An over-zealous marketing manager can produce a pressure of unsatisfied demand which, particularly in transport, forces the hand of general management to push up production beyond the optimum point. The danger exists because in the transport industry a business rarely faces a 'market-price'. The idea of a market-price takes us back to the simple market-place buying and selling. In a market-place there tends to be *one price*, that results from the inter-reaction of all the buyers and sellers in the market. Seldom does an individual dominate the market in the sense that he can choose to charge what price he likes within fairly wide limits. On the other hand, the individual supplier tends not to have to lower his price to increase his sales. He is able to sell all that he can supply at the prevailing market-price, just because he is too small a fish to have an effect on price.

Usually there are not enough suppliers in the transport market, nor are the various forms of transport sufficiently alike to give rise to a market-price. Each transport business tends to dominate its particular market to such an extent that *the amount it supplies will affect price*, and, therefore, it can sell an increased supply of its transport only by reducing the price prevailing for all similar transport. The prices of transport businesses are referred to as 'monopolistic'. This term can be misleading because it suggests a business facing no competition, whereas almost all transport businesses face some competition, But few of them have a cohesive body of competitors to compel the acceptance of a single, all-pervading price.

Managements who frame marketing policies, based on monopolistic prices, are not as independent and as powerful as they are commonly believed to be. There are two variables in marketing: the first is price; the second is the amount sold. Whichever variable management chooses to control, it must leave control of the other variable in the hands of buyers. If the management of a transport undertaking fixes prices, customers will decide how much they will buy at those prices. If management decides it will aim to sell a certain quantity of transport, implicitly the decision means at any price, and customers will decide the price at which they are willing to take up the amount on offer. However, management's inability to control both variables does not preclude success in business. The control of one variable is sufficient to enable managements to frame businesslike marketing policies.

The position in transport is, however, sometimes worse than this. Sometimes the community attempts to deny management the right to control either of the variables. This is when the community tries to say 'how much' transport shall be provided, and at 'what price'. This applies particularly to nationalised transport undertakings. Confirmation can be found in comments in the course of a closer definition, proposed for the financial and economic obligations of these undertakings in the 1961 White Paper,[1]

'. . . the fact of nationalisation has tended to arouse public expectation that the products and services of these industries should be provided cheaply, and the Boards have been continuously subject to pressure from public opinion to keep their own prices down even when costs and prices elsewhere have been rising'.

'. . . if the prices of the goods and services which the nationalised industries provide are uneconomically low, demand for them (and for investment to produce more of them) may be artificially stimulated'.

But nationalisation cannot be held to blame for all the lack of businesslike pricing policies in the major transport undertakings. For a long period before nationalisation our railways made

[1] The Financial and Economic Obligations of the Nationalised Industries, Cmnd. 1337, HMSO.

practically no use of the pricing tools of marketing. An appendix to the Select Committee Report of 1960 on the 'Commercial Outlook' of British Railways said:

'It is only a few years since the idea of railways as an ordinary commercial business, charging according to "cost" and "market" rather than by publicly-regulated schemes of rates, and basing themselves on policies which must be discriminating and competitive at all points, came into being. However much the facts of the situation had changed since the days before the first World War, especially in the world of freight transport, theoretically the railways were still a closely-regulated monopoly sitting at the receipt of custom, and their internal organisation and their methods of charging were virtually unchanged. The adjustments needed in selling organisation and techniques after the 1953 Act were in some ways as great and decisive as the physical modernisation required.'

and subsequently commented on the changes in sales organisation in these words:

'. . . At the same time the organisation for study and research into traffic matters, including market surveys, commercial intelligence and costing and rate questions, has been built up and expanded. All in all a considerable process of indoctrination, training and experiment has gone forward. A lively and sophisticated type of organisation is emerging in which the key figure is the new traffic manager or commercial man, who is ready to take responsibilities and weigh results and is able to meet on level terms the local leaders of commerce and public life.'

This leads us naturally to the crux of the commercial attitude in marketing management, that is the task of drawing attention to the wares. The task calls for a vigorous, extrovert, showmanlike outlook. This is not to say that these are the personal qualities required of a marketing manager, but that he must infuse sufficient of these qualities into the whole organisation to make it businesslike. It is not just a matter of the marketing manager making his own departmental employees display-conscious, but also of instilling into finance, purchasing, production, personnel and research and development men the fact that they all work for or against the attainment of the goal of attractive display. There is really no neutral position in this respect. During the 1960's report after report stressed the need for transport management to take a more commercial attitude towards publicity.

Typical of the advice given are the following comments made in the Report of the Committee of Inquiry into the Major Ports of Great Britain, September 1962 (Cmnd. 1824 HMSO), on the subjects of 'Commercial management and publicity'.

'. . . one criticism we had received related to the lack of emphasis on commercial management. We think there is some substance in this criticism and that British port authorities could generally do more to promote business by taking the initiative in discussing with shippers, hauliers and forwarding agents how best to meet their requirements and iron out their difficulties. Commercial superintendents can play a big part here and their position in the management structure should, if necessary, be strengthened to assist them to do so. Not all ports employ commercial superintendents; where the size of the port merits it we think such an officer should be appointed.'

'. . . There is also the question of publicising ports' facilities and advantages. As our foreign trade expands it is increasingly important that our port literature should be as attractive and informative as possible. We think that most British ports would do well to emulate the high standard set by the major near Continental and United States ports in this respect. There will increasingly be a need for port handbooks to be published in more than one language.'

These comments raise points of vital importance to the success of the 'drawing attention' or 'display' aspect of marketing management. Firstly, success depends upon an aggressive, not passive, attitude to the subject. Secondly, marketing management must be given sufficient authority in organisation. It should rank equally with finance, production management and so on. Thirdly, marketing management must put pen to paper to produce attractive and informative literature. Pamphleteering is now a firmly established marketing practice.

Finally, having established the need for a positive approach to the marketing function in transport, we must acknowledge, that in highly developed communities, successful marketing is better based on an intelligent understanding and exploitation of what is, rather than the attitude of pioneering. There may still be a place for the latter, but in general there are few surprises left for transport managers in highly developed communities. This conclusion is not meant in any way to denigrate the efforts of market research in transport. We need to find out certain facts to provide a basis for an intelligent approach to the marketing task of transport management. What is discovered should guide business spending on advertising, sales promotion literature, and disposition of sales force. But we will be disappointed if we look for startling discoveries. Much of market research does a good job in merely confirming what we already suspect; only marginally does it pull a surprise out of the hat. When it does, it may provide a very valuable marginal advantage.

The author set out in the early 1950's to discover the extent to which the marketing of air transport in the United States had been dominated by social and political influences; the extent to which it had been allowed to respond freely to geographical and economic influences; and the extent to which it had reflex effects on social and economic trends.[1]

The development of United States airlines was in some ways hampered by the passing of the Civil Aeronautics Act 1938. Growth up to 1938 was not in accordance with any clear national plan or policy. It was guided mainly by ideas inspired by the role that ground and water transport had assumed in the production and population patterns of the United States. After 1938 the development of airlines suffered from a preoccupation with the concept of 'the air transportation system of the United States'. While, in theory, federal regulation was to have the broadest aims of encouraging and developing an air transport system properly adapted to the present and future needs of foreign and domestic commerce, the postal service and the national defence of the United States, in fact, the 'grandfather' awards of 1938, dominated airlines for a long time.

Air routes had been fitted into regions that were the right size for successful railways, and extension of original awards had

[1] Air Transport in the United States: a study in the economic geography of the growth and function of selected airlines. Thesis, University of London, 1954.

been frustrated by antipathy to nation-wide monopolies. The worst abuses of uncontrolled competition were checked, but there was failure to conceive a national plan readily allowing speedy changes to be made, to keep pace with technical progress in a transport medium so characteristically different from its predecessors. Legislative and administrative processes, working within the arbitrary divisions of United States air transport into Domestic, Territorial and Foreign Services, had further entrenched the idea that the domestic routes allotted were economic units for airline operations.

Federal policies had not been readily accepted by the airlines. It was evident that some of them, in seeking the optimum (marketing) unit, regarded their domestic bases as a series of terminals at one end of an inter-continental service. Many of them had widely used the freedom allowed them within confines so apparently arbitrary and inadequate for economic service, by varying the links among the authorised stops, that were the basis of the original share-out. Use of the permissive power to make through flights was, however, a freedom that could be checked by the Civil Aeronautics Board's authority to compel adequate service at any base.

The population pattern of the United States had generally become so stable that airlines were compelled for many years to accept the existing large centres for the provision of most of their traffic. The only important current increase of population in the south-west, although not caused by air transport, might have been assisted by it. The United States had no 'bush' operations like those in Canada, with their pronounced reflex effects on population trends. Some United States airlines had experimented in serving small communities, but nowhere was there evidence that these provisions had brought about exceptional growth in population.

The process of fitting air transport into the pattern of United States economy was still far from complete. In the development of airlines, provision of passenger and mail services had taken first place. The influence of administrative, tourist and trading centres on traffic had so far exceeded that of production centres, but it was too early to judge what the final effect of the latter would be. Current trends suggested that freight would be handled by companies specialising in this form of traffic, since freight-carrying problems were so different from those of passenger and mail services. That might have avoided the uneconomic compromises implicit in a combination of the two functions in one airline.

The costliness of air transport made it more sensitive than surface transport to irregularities in demand that were too often the product of unsuitable shape and layout. High crew costs and high power costs per unit (from heavy consumption of expensive fuel against a relatively small weight of payload) were the two main items contributing to heavy direct running costs. Firstly, then, high running costs, added to heavy overheads against small payloads, made it necessary for each passenger to pay highly for service. He thus had a greater economic importance individually than in any other mode of transport. Secondly, because running costs were so heavy, the critical point between profitable and unprofitable operation on each flight was much nearer the maximum payload than for any other form of transport. As a result, air transport was very sensitive to marginal movements of passengers. It was to be regretted that this had been so little appreciated when shape and layout were crystallised by the 'grandfather' awards, as non-revenue flights, and radical changes of direction were serious problems on some airline routes.

Perhaps one of the greatest difficulties confronting the new medium was to fit into production and population patterns, with communities of interest built up by carriers profitably operating very much shorter stages than those suitable for aircraft. Ideally aircraft stops should be spaced at a distance apart that approximates to the optimum length of stage for the aircraft in use. This was difficult to achieve in the face of demand for service neither fashioned by the technical characteristics of aircraft, nor responsive to rapid progress in aircraft design. Added to this there was the ever-present political threat that lay in the power of the federal authorities to compel 'adequate' service at intermediate halts.

Bad weather accentuating the operating difficulties of airlines in different areas of the continent, was one of the main obstacles in attempts to standardise domestic passenger fares and freight charges. With the existing division of airline routes, the behaviour of climate and weather had either to be reflected in a variety of charges per mile of air travel, or be masked by differential mail subsidies. The latter course gave rise to recurrent wrangles for increased subsidies, and was accompanied by the fear that bad management would be sustained by what was properly compensation for adverse geographical conditions.

A study of the relationships between schedules and the topography of areas served by certain selected airlines had emphasised the sensitivity of air transport to rail competition. There had been a resulting tendency for airlines to assume the function of providing through services and neglecting point to point traffic where topography made for keen rail competition. The amount of time-saving provided by airlines was increased by reducing the number of halts aircraft made. The practice was fundamentally a limited endeavour to make flight stages approach their optimum length in a population pattern unfavourable in this respect.

Another interesting trend in the marketing of air transport, was the attempt to extend its function beyond that of providing alternative means of transport between traditional communities of interest. Up to this point the new medium had been fitted into an existing pattern. It used the major centres of population as the main supply of traffic, and was apparently not responsible for the growth of new centres. Most of the evidence pointed to the fact that it was more shaped by, than shaping, the existing economic pattern. In adhering to the conventional pattern of communications, airlines had been compelled to face increased costs resulting from short distances between one town and another, and adverse meteorological conditions that place them even more at the mercy of their competitors.

But the provision of new arteries of communication might have created new communities of interest, free from the keenest rail competition. These departures from orthodox lines took advantage of the aircraft's freedom from the effects of surface obstacles. If successful they might have produced important reflex effects on population and production patterns. But to be successful airlines must change habits of travel powerfully entrenched over a period of more than two centuries.

While it was too early to assess the probable success of these ventures, it was possible at that stage to observe some related trends.

Firstly, it was clear that airlines were not disposed to rely for their future prosperity on an extension of this function. Pressure was constantly being exerted on the Civil Aeronautics Board to authorise extensions and amalgamations. Thus, the basin of the Mississippi, which had proved to be a satisfactory economic unit for at least three railways, had not been regarded as such by Chicago and Southern. In 1953 a merger was announced between Chicago and Southern and Delta Airlines (another pioneer airline). Delta, with 24 years of experience in serving the South and linking it with the Midwest, joined with Chicago and Southern, which had served the Mississippi Valley for 19 years. The merger tied mid-America to the West Indies and South America.

Trends in airline marketing in the United States between 1945 and 1955 were illustrative of characteristics of marketing in other forms of transport. First of all a transport system, whether it be crystallised by permanent way or government licence, in a highly developed community is something of a marketing straight-jacket. Economic-geographical factors shape the marketing within the system. Alternative marketing policies influence the general pattern only marginally. Aggressive marketing management seeks not so much to change population and economic conditions within the production system, but to change or extend the production system as a means of re-fashioning the market. Devices for extending the production system to widen the market include, of course, increases in organisation (laying new permanent tracks, more vehicles or more traffic rights), but also mergers to consortia of carriers.

One way of loosening the bonds of the transport system straight-jacket on marketing is by the development of 'off-line' sales. This is where people who live well outside a carrier's marketing area are sold tickets on its services, when they are booking passages to bring them within the marketing area. For example, someone going into a travel agent to book a sea-passage to New York may, at the same time, buy rail tickets for a journey by a certain railroad from New York to Chicago.

And this brings us to the role of the travel agent in transport marketing. Much of the skill in marketing management in transport lies in the way that relations with travel agents are handled. How does a marketing manager persuade agents to sell the transport produced by his particular business? Some concealed form of bribery might do for a while. But in the long run there is no substitute for the due care and attention given to the agents' clients. In a sense travel agents magnify both good and bad treatment of customers by carriers. The bad treatment of a travel agent's client may lose the carrier not just one person's custom, but the whole of an agent's contribution to the business. The relationship between the carrier's marketing management and the travel agent is one of partnership in the goodwill of customers.

CHAPTER XVII

PERSONNEL MANAGEMENT IN TRANSPORT UNDERTAKINGS

Personnel management in any business is concerned with ideas of justice and fair play. Different people's ideas of what is just and what is fair do not always agree, but there is usually enough agreement to make personnel management practicable. Men do not like being treated badly *compared with* other men. For example, they do not like to have advantages over other workers, as expressed in pay differentials, reduced by raising the pay of lower grades. This they regard as being treated comparatively badly. They argue that it is unfair to single out one grade of worker for improvement in pay: everyone must be treated equally.

Managers may not agree with operatives' ideas on fair play, but the fact of their existence may be a lot more important than their wrongness. While management does not have to *accept* wrong ideas on what is just and fair, this does not mean that they can ignore them. Employees' ideas on fair play are often traditional, and traditions cannot be treated lightly.

It takes time to weigh up the changing patterns of working in a thriving business; time to weigh up the effects on the working lives of human beings; time that business production or sales managers cannot afford to spare. And so it is advisable, in a business of any size, for one manager to be set aside to give thought to these issues.

The maintenance of good internal relations, concerning how one man stands with another, is not just a matter of preserving the *status quo*. Personnel management has many and varied tasks, which are briefly:

(*a*) recruiting people to achieve few square pegs in round holes,
(*b*) equipping people with skills and knowledge,

(*c*) minimising waste of human talent,
(*d*) giving business a 'memory' of human resources in records,
(*e*) checking processes that threaten to outstrip human capabilities,
(*f*) protecting business from false grievances, wilful indiscipline and incompetence,
(*g*) handling industrial relations,
(*h*) constructing a just wage structure,
(*i*) ensuring that working surroundings are fit for human beings,
(*j*) ensuring that 'fringe' benefits are matched to the real needs of workers and the capacity of the business.

All these ingredients are required in transport. But just as in any other business, the policies of personnel management need to be shaped to fit the business. The transport characteristics that produce key areas may be summarised as follows:

(*a*) intermittent work,
(*b*) mixed mechanical and social skills,
(*c*) dispersal of operatives, geographically and in time.

Intermittent work

One of the features of employment in transport is the intermittent nature of work, particularly at terminals and bases. Work is not regular and at a pace controlled by the individual worker. Captain Lincoln Lee, in his book entitled *Three-Dimensioned Darkness*,[1] refers to the job of a pilot as, 'Years of boredom, punctuated by moments of panic'. Although it was made about work in vehicles, this remark indicates the extreme of the situation at terminals.

There is no single cause of the intermittent nature. Some of it is due to conditions outside the control of the industry. For example, fluctuations of trade from time of recession to time of boom, or from summer to winter, from weekday to weekend, from day to night, may produce irregularities in the flow of traffic. Random factors, like storms at sea delaying the arrival of ships, may bring idleness to terminals. On the other hand, some causes lie within the control of the industry, but not within the control of the individual worker. Indeed, production

[1] George Allen & Unwin Limited, 1962.

management aims at keeping vehicles on the move and at spending minimum time at terminals. Vehicle 'turn-round' times are constantly reviewed for possible improvements. Optimum production conditions of vehicles on the move, and minimum turn-round times at terminals, make for short bursts of maximum activity and long periods of idleness. In sea and air transport, terminals can have vehicles coming in and going out all day, keeping terminal authorities busy, without affecting the intermittent nature of work of individual carriers.

A similar situation may prevail in maintenance bases. Activity may be feverish during checks and repairs, with everyone going all out to get a vehicle back into service. Then comes the waiting-time. This waiting-time—waiting for vehicles to arrive, for work to arrive—is not helpful in promoting good relations between management and operatives.

The extreme of ill-effects is seen in the situation in dockyards. The system of casual employment of dock labour is notorious. The Report of the Committee of Inquiry into the Major Ports of Great Britain (Cmnd. 1824, HMSO 1962) said:

'Apart from the minority of weekly workers, i.e. those employed on a semi-permanent basis, the dock labour force is still essentially a casual one. The daily workers assemble twice daily to obtain work, the intervals between the first and second "calls" varying from port to port.'

The Dock Labour Board had been set up to alleviate some of the worst aspects of casual labour. It was a clearing-house for ensuring that available men were matched to available work. However, by 1961, the scheme had not done much to 'decasualise' labour. In 1951 there were 13,500 *weekly* workers; by 1961 this had been increased to 16,500. The rise of 3,000 was a small proportion of the total of 70,000 employed as dock labourers in 1961. Despite the 'free-call' system of some ports, e.g. London, where the men themselves met the employers and engaged themselves for work, a man might still have had a dozen or so different employers in a week. Therefore, there was no permanent relationship between one employee and one employer. There was no chance of building up mutual trust and understanding. The Committee went on to say:

'Casual employment breeds casual attitudes, and so long as the casual labour system persists and there are times when men have no regular work and only the consolation of "fall-back pay", the situation is always potentially ripe for the exploitation of discontent. It seems to us beyond doubt that such exploitation has in the past taken place and that conditions have made it possible for strikes to be fomented despite the efforts of the unions to avoid them. It is not enough, in our view, to say that the unions must achieve more influence, though it is indeed vitally important that trade-union organisation should be effective, especially at the lower levels, and that communications between union officials and members should be good: the right atmosphere must be created in which that influence can be exercised.'

An important point is made here. Neither the influence of trade unions, nor the influence of personnel management is exercised in a vacuum. They must both be exercised in some sort of 'atmosphere', good or bad, that results from working conditions. It is not practicable to use personnel officers as a device for smoothing ruffled feelings caused by inhuman processes of production. A personnel officer is no more capable than anyone else of making a fundamentally bad situation look good.

Why does waiting-time create a bad atmosphere in the internal relations of a business? First, there are cases where men are paid either nothing, or less than average (as 'fall-back', 'flat-rate' or 'basic' pay), when they are on waiting-time. This appears unfair to operatives who do not ask for spasmodic work that time and tide force upon them. They cannot control trade, or the arrival of ships or aircraft, that play ducks and drakes with their household budget. It is fairly easy for managers to see the logic of a no-work, no-pay situation, but it is not easy for men on the shop floor who believe that men who are willing to work have a right to it. Their wives probably prefer lower regular earnings to higher irregular earnings.

If men recognise that the harder they work when work is available, the longer their idle periods will be, there will be dissatisfaction. The best personnel policy in this situation may not be that of stimulating by bonuses further effort during working periods, to be followed by longer periods on fall-back pay. However old-fashioned it sounds, the truth is that idleness is bad for all that we loosely call morale. Good morale in business is a spirit engendered by the business that raises men's conduct above the level of their conduct as individuals. Bad morale makes them do bad things that they would not do as individuals. Good morale makes them do good things that they would not do as individuals. Men do not, at heart, like wasting time at work. It irritates them. Complete inactivity is virtually impossible, either physically or mentally, and denied legitimate outlet for their energies men turn to mischief. So the soundest personnel policy is to aim at the elimination of waiting-time, by the provision of alternative employment. This is easier said than done, but the problem is not insurmountable. We might envy the ease with which country railway stationmasters solve their problems by cultivating track-side gardens.

Efforts to keep men in dockyards employed on whatever work is available is frustrated by there being nearly a hundred occupational groups within port organisation. Restrictive practices thrive among lines of demarcation. These reduce the mobility of labour and accentuate the problem of overcoming intermittent employment. Once they have gained a grip in organisation, restrictive practices are extremely difficult to root out. Their prevention is much easier than their cure. Personnel policy should be geared to prevent the multiplication of occupational groups; once established, such groups begin to carve out exclusive areas of work.

The personnel policy necessary to counteract the tendencies to intermittent employment in transport undertakings may be summarised as follows:

(1) Encourage methods of organisation to even out flow of work:

- (*a*) by off-peak production and off-peak training,
- (*b*) by promoting mobility of labour,
- (*c*) by preventing narrow job specification.

(2) Minimise the effect of unavoidable irregularities in flow of work:

- (*a*) by devising a wage structure that avoids penalising men through no fault of their own.

(*b*) by preventing the wage structure from emphasising the distress of waiting-time. Waiting-time should be better paid, and not worse paid in some parts of organisation,

(*c*) by fostering a new attitude towards waiting-time in general, drawing attention to the skills of maintaining states of readiness.

Mixed Mechanical and Social Skills

There is a tendency in transport undertakings for ever-increasing doses of 'technical' training. By technical is meant the advanced mechanical skills of maintenance and vehicle handling. There is a need for more training due to complexity of equipment. But there are dangers of having too much. Also with intensification of pride of calling, academic entry qualifications become more and more exacting. These trends may lead to disproportionate demands that are self-defeating, because young people with these qualifications may prefer wider opportunities, following studies at university.

There are two main problems in industrial training; the first is economic, and the second psychological. As in other spheres of human activity, money spent on training is subject to diminishing returns. This is not technically significant until operations are reasonably safe, but beyond this point business-like assessments of training should take over. The psychological dangers of excessive technical training are recognisable in staleness, loss of initiative, and other signs of mental indigestion. The effects of excessive technical training are magnified by the reduction in resources available for other forms of training, as for elementary mechanical skills (like the loading and unloading of vehicles), and for training in social skills that are of importance in transport. Technical training is usually increased at the cost of 'non-technical' training. This unbalancing is soon reflected in the standards of performance on the line. Customers then discover that some operatives are well trained, and some badly trained. Personnel management should advise on the balanced disposal of resources for training.

Training is a difficult activity to control. In few cases is it possible to measure its effectiveness with precision. Those concerned with industrial training are often amateurs, uncertain of themselves, and inclined to play safe by doing more training rather than less. One way of establishing managerial control is by inspection—a form of control that has existed in other training and educational fields for a long time. Poor training techniques that would be revealed by an efficient inspectorate are:

(*a*) the use of 'gimmicks' in instruction, and adherence to fashion in techniques,
(*b*) the excessive use of simulation, by 'chinese' copies that imitate reality to no purpose,
(*c*) the neglect of basic teaching skills,
(*d*) different standards from one area to another.

The need for inspection of industrial training calls for the employment of qualified specialists in teaching. Without a specialist, general management can easily be deceived as to the real need for training.

After this cautionary note on the difficulties of managerial control, we may deal with the importance of training to a transport undertaking. There is an obvious need in the case of certain operatives. Grants of licences to pilots, of ships and aircraft, and to maintenance engineers, are dependent upon their having reached a certain standard of performance, and this creates an inescapable need. On the other hand, there is escapable but necessary training to make an undertaking *competitive*. A lot of traffic may be lost to British ports because of poor manual skill, that results in mishandled and damaged cargo. During 1961 London and Liverpool began training schemes on the lines of the Rotterdam training school for dockers. These workers need training to create pride-in-calling. Other grades already have over-developed pride-in-calling.

Training for social skills is necessary to give transport undertakings a commercial outlook. In the mixture of skills that concern the customer we must avoid allowing the mechanical to exclude the social.

Dispersal of operatives, geographically and in time

Geographical dispersal of operatives makes it difficult to control standards of working conditions. If workpeople are gathered under a factory roof, their conditions attract the attention of unions, and management find economic justification for good conditions. Amenities tend to be regarded worthwhile if they are enjoyed by a number of people. Suggestions for doing something to benefit a few are not so well received. Expenditure on amenities for workpeople is likely to be judged on *cost per head*, rather than on any other basis.

Good working conditions can be costly for transport undertakings with small groups of men spread out over a network. This was not the reason for the situation in the docks up to 1960, because here we had large concentrations of workpeople. But there was an idea that it was not necessary to bother so much about people who worked in the open air: it was only when they were shut up in factories that they needed protection. The Minister of Labour had powers under the Factories Acts to make regulations for the welfare of dockworkers, although the minimum detailed standards laid down in the Acts did not apply to docks. The Public Health Act of 1936 put certain responsibility on to the Ministry of Housing and Local Government for providing sanitary accommodation. However, the 1948 Working Party on Turn-Round of Shipping in United Kingdom Ports said of personnel management in the dockyards:

'Much remains to be done, however, particularly with regard to amenities and working conditions. In this respect docks generally compare unfavourably with many industrial establishments and present a drab picture. Often the layout is not only very unattractive, but does not allow of the best methods of working. Sanitary accommodation is frequently of a deplorably low standard. Feeding arrangements are not always satisfactory, and the quality of the service in the canteens varies considerably. Washing facilities are in many cases quite inadequate and more drying and changing rooms are needed. It is also essential that there should be adequate industrial medical services.'

Related to the problems of providing decent working conditions for small units of men spread over a transport network, are those of providing amenities for men who have to live on the job and away from home. For centuries working conditions in ships were bad. Almost every aspect of human consideration was sacrificed to sailing distance, speed, safety and fighting power. This was understandable for an era in which it needed all man's cleverness to survive at sea, let alone be comfortable. But since those days working conditions, fit for human beings, have had to be enforced by statute.

To this day insufficient thought is given to the design of bridges, or cockpits, or drivers' cabins, from the point of view of the human beings who work in them. Human ingenuity tends to be concentrated on performance standards of engines and vehicles frames.

In railways and airlines there are frequent complaints about the standard of 'lodgings' for vehicle crews while they are away from home. In some companies standards of accommodation are generally high, but spoiled by a few black spots. It is careless management to acquire a bad reputation for the sake of marginal provisions. On the other hand, some vehicle crews make unreasonable demands, and their grievances are more in the nature of testing the strength of management, rather than genuine expressions of discontent.

In national and international networks there is the problem of giving equal treatment to operatives doing the same job in different environments. The cost of living may differ from one city to another, and even more from one country to another. Items regarded as necessary in the budget of a family in the south may not be the same as those regarded as necessary in the north, and vice versa. Usually international carriers are compelled to adjust basic rates of pay by superimposing a complicated scale of allowances that differs from one country to another. National rates are not usually so adjusted, although the higher cost of living in big conurbations is made up by an allowance, e.g. a 'London' allowance. If pay is not equalised from one area to another the disparities will tend to encourage immobility of labour. A man whose £15 a week is worth more in the provinces will think hard before he goes to London for fresh experience.

Then there is the problem of compensating for, and alleviating the ill-effects, of the dispersal of operatives in time, by shift-working. Working when other people are enjoying themselves or sleeping, puts a person out of step with his fellows. It even keeps him out of step with members of his own family. At best it drives him to seek the company of his fellow shift-workers, and at worst makes him lonely. A changing shift-pattern, say nights for one week, and days for the next week, is even more disruptive of family and social life, as the worker then has a foot in two camps, and in neither very satisfactorily. Add irregularity to change, and we have the worst of all combinations. An irregular and changing shift pattern almost brings normal family and social life to a standstill. A person who does not know where he will be in a week or a fortnight's time cannot arrange his life in a normal fashion.

People who work irregular shift patterns lead unstable lives. We might expect to find among them more neuroses, more broken marriages and other domestic troubles. We might also expect them to be a little sensitive in their relations within organisation. Their circumstances call for patience and understanding. Perhaps the most dangerous aspect of abnormal ways of living is that people do not experience the usual maturing processes of living. Divorce from the common or garden run of life tends to result in immaturity.

A feature of shift-work often overlooked is the effect on the continued education of employees. Workers on night-shift may well be cut off from adult education in its broadest sense. This may be serious for a worker needing to repair gaps in his education, or wishing to gain technical or professional qualifications. Some companies alleviate this position by financing studies with correspondence colleges, or by running their own company correspondence courses. KLM, the Royal Dutch Airlines have a well-developed correspondence school for sales training, not designed specifically to overcome this problem, but indicative of what can be done by way of company tuition.

CHAPTER XVIII

RESEARCH AND DEVELOPMENT

James Watt's fundamental improvements in the steam-engine were among the early scientific efforts that gave rise to new businesses. Railways have their beginnings in a small workshop in Glasgow University in the 1750's. And Watt had similar difficulties in developing ideas produced by his research as many discoverers and inventors have to this day.

In Britain, the value of research to industry was recognised in 1900 by the opening of the National Physical Laboratory. It set out to standardise and test materials and instruments used in industry. Among its eight divisions are several whose work has contributed to the solution of problems in transport. Two of these divisions have dealt directly with transport problems, through research in aerodynamics and ships. The NPL was taken over in 1918 by the Department of Scientific and Industrial Research, which had been formed in 1915 as a result of wartime needs of industry.

The research establishments controlled by the DSIR aim to work in fields that affect the community at large, rather than specific industries. Hence there is emphasis on food, fuel, road conditions and so on. Nevertheless, the work of these establishments is often important to individual businesses.

The Government came to the conclusion at the time the DSIR was set up that research on problems concerning clearly defined industries should be conducted and controlled by the industries themselves. So a scheme for the formation of a number of research associations, in which both government and industry would play a part, was launched in 1916. By 1920 twenty-three of these associations had been formed, and by 1960 the number had risen to forty. The aim of each Research Association is to bring the benefits of science to its particular industry. While these Associations differ from one to another there are activities common to most of them. The sort of research they set out to do is not usually fundamental, but it may often create a need for some new basic scientific knowledge, and the Associations often turn to universities for this, although the former are tending to tackle more fundamental work themselves. To assist in the programmes of research there is usually an intelligence service and reference library. Then the associations usually have a development department to bridge the gap between the laboratory and the factory floor. Sometimes the staff of the development departments of the RA's go down on to the shop floor and set up pilot plant demonstrations. Associations often have technical information sections to assist the work of the development department (i.e. separate from the information section attached to the research department). Lastly, some of the Associations send their scientists out into industry to study working methods. Industrial research is tending to include more and more of the human factor, and to branch into such studies as those of human comfort, fatigue and economy of movement.

Research Associations whose work may have some bearing on transport problems are:

British Cast Iron RA
British Ceramics RA
British Coal Utilisation RA
British Electrical and Allied Industries RA
British Glass Industry RA
Heating & Ventilating Research Council
British Hydromechanics RA
British Internal Combustion Engine RA
British Iron & Steel RA
Parsons & Marine Engineering Turbine R&DA
Motor Industry RA
British Non-Ferrous Metals RA
British Paint, Colour and Varnish Manufacturers RA
Production Engineering RA
British Scientific Instruments RA
British Shipbuilding RA
British Steel Castings RA
British Welding RA

Under the Ministry of Aviation there is the famous Royal Aircraft Establishment at Farnborough, with sections dealing with aircraft equipment, engines, air-frames, scientific matters (air), and electronics.

In 1960 Mr Macmillan appointed Lord Hailsham to be Lord Privy Seal and the first Minister of Science and Technology, with responsibility for a number of research bodies, among them the DSIR. This set the seal on the Government's recognition of the vital necessity of the application of science to industry for the sake of the prosperity of the whole country. In general British industry has been slow to appreciate the value of highly educated people in its ranks, and it had to be coaxed along by governments, first to the stage of co-operative research, as we see in the Research Associations, and then to the stage of employing scientists within individual companies.

The Committee of Inquiry into the Major Ports of Great Britain (1962) said:

'We are convinced that insufficient resources are today devoted by the port industry to scientific research and development in all fields of port activity. For instance, there seems to be a need for research into such matters as dredging, forward planning of such operations as the arrival of lorries at the docks, the provision of cranes (including heavy lift equipment), the cost of "idle time" of ships lying in dock, ways and means of increasing output with the existing facilities and labour force, the extent to which throughput can be economically increased by providing additional facilities, etc.'

The Committee prefixed the term 'research and development' by the word 'scientific'. Some research in the transport industry is not scientific. That may not matter: there are ways of establishing facts other than by scientific method. Deductive methods, judicial methods, and even casual observations are adequate in certain circumstances. But it does matter if the circumstances call for the use of scientific method.

Management must be equipped to distinguish the genuine from the false in scientific investigation. They may have a scientist in the management team, specialising in research and development. Short of this they may commission outside research institutions to do work. If R and D is brought into organisation it must be done thoroughly or it is more of a danger than a help.

We should note the sort of problems the Committee referred to as being suitable subjects for research. We might be surprised, for example, to see dredging, and idle ships, in the list. This points to the need for managements with minds alert to the possible benefits of scientific investigation.

Some research needs to be conducted on an industry-wide basis, rather than by an individual undertaking. Some of it calls for resources that no single business can command. Some findings would be helpful to all businesses in the industry, so it would be unfair if one business shouldered all the cost, and wasteful if several engaged on the same research. There is more room for co-ordinated research in the industry. The Dock Committee applauded the decision of the British National Committees of the International Cargo Handling Co-ordination Association and the Permanent International Association of Navigation Congresses to set up a Joint Committee on cargo handling. The Dock Committee went on to recommend the setting up of a Port Industry Research Association, but warned against allowing it to grow too big, too quickly; rather hand some of the studies over to specialist research organisations like the British Ship Research Association, the Building Research Station, the Hydraulics Station, the British Iron and Steel Research Association and the British Standards Institution.

An important part of R and D management involves the decision whether to conduct a piece of research within organisation, or to do it by contracting to a specialist research organisation. A nicety of judgement is often involved in weighing the relative advantages of industrial expertise against research expertise. It is important for R and D management to keep abreast of work going on outside its business.

All forms of transport have some relevant specialist research organisations to whom they may contract. For European air carriers there is the Air Research Bureau in Brussels, for road transport in Britain there is the Road Research Laboratory, and so on. On the other hand, some forms of transport have development branches within their own business organisation. The two nationalised air corporations have ploughed a lot of money into development. But the efforts of the late

British Transport Commission were not impressive, in either field.

The Commission relied on suppliers to conduct research in their own fields, but acknowledged the need for some effort within the BTC organisation. It had been found that suppliers' research, aimed at increasing sales, did not always help the aim of the Commission, say to reduce maintenance costs. Problems concerning the interaction of vehicle and track, stresses in rails, corrosion, snags in maintenance, and the interaction of equipment supplied by different manufacturers were fields in which the Commission had been compelled to do its own research. Even where manufacturers had undertaken long-term design projects, the Commission had found it necessary to recruit technically qualified staff to discuss matters with them.

Out of a total annual working expenditure of £750 million the British Transport Commission was spending about £2 million on Research and Development. Of this £2 million, approximately £700,000 was being spent on research, and the remaining £1,300,000 on engineering development. Much of the £700,000 was, on the Commission's own admission, spent on day-to-day advice and investigation on routine matters. 90 per cent of the so-called research expenditure was spent on the railways, and the remaining 10 per cent had to be shared by the other Divisions of the Commission. The Commission's reasons for devoting such a small proportion of their revenue to research and development was declared in 1960 to be because, firstly, their primary function was to provide a transport service, not to manufacture; and secondly, their suppliers were undertaking research and development. From reading between the lines it was not difficult to realise that this activity had been neglected and much remained to be done. During the same period the Japanese railways were spending over double the sum spent by British Railways on research.

Just before the British Transport Commission was abolished, the British Railways Division began to get under way with research programmes. New engineering laboratories and research headquarters were built at Derby, and there began a series of studies that promised well for technical progress. Vacuum brakes and disc brakes for freight and passenger trains, the mechanics of track formation failures, wagon control, paint finishes, signal relays all figured in current programmes. The railways were also turning to computers as possible means of preparing railways timetables. The Railways Operational Research Unit had contracted with Leeds University for the use of its computer in the search for a mathematical method for determining the optimum scheduling of locomotives and train crews. At the same time the University of Liverpool was asked to do a similar study for the Tilling Group. With the help of computers, linear programming techniques were applied to a study of the distribution of empty wagons. Another link with university research departments was to be found in a study begun at University College, London on the fundamental dynamics of the motion of a railway vehicle on a track.

An example of progress in development work on the railways was the building and equipping of the Locomotive, Carriage and Wagon Development Unit.

The highest level at which research and development was promoted in the British Transport Commission, was in the Technical Committee (composed of members of the Commission). The Technical Committee was assisted by a Research Advisory Council (composed of authorities from universities and industry). The R and D 'manager' was a Chief of Research who was directly responsible to the Commission. The duties of the Chief of Research included the preparation and submission of research programmes and annual budgets, for consideration by the Technical Committee. He was also responsible for seeing that the results of research were carried forward into the field of development. He was assisted by a Research Co-ordination Committee, and an Advisory Panel on Electronic Computing and Control Devices.

In road transport, research was being undertaken into low viscosity oils for lubrication, fuel consumption, exhaust smoke, strain gauge techniques, polyster gas laminates, rail de-icing, tyre testing, etc. In docks and waterways research, such subjects as bank protection, pollution, silting, dock gate corrosion, and design of barges were studied.

In the shipping industry a good deal of research is done co-operatively by shipbuilders. Most United Kingdom shipbuilders belong to a trade association called the Shipbuilding Conference. In 1944 the Conference worked with the Department of Scientific and Industrial Research to form the British

Shipbuilding Research Association. This provided an industry-wide research effort. It made it possible to conduct large-scale research co-operatively and thus made possible projects that would otherwise not have been contemplated, as they would have caused too heavy a financial burden for individual firms. On the other hand, a good deal of research is done by the bigger individual firms like Vickers.

Is enough spent on research and development in the British transport industry by all agencies—Department of Industrial Research (government), Universities (independent), Research Associations (co-operative by numbers of firms in the industry), and individual companies? It is difficult to make reliable estimates despite the fact that a large part of the industry is publicly owned, but we would be unwise in the absence of evidence to take a complacent view. Insufficient R and D in a domestic business will result in customers getting a poorer service. Insufficient R and D in an international transport business will result in its becoming uncompetitive.

A question that often arises is who should pay for research and development? Should the manufacturer of vehicles, or route equipment, or terminal equipment, pay for the R and D he has to do? Or should the R and D be paid for by the government on the grounds that it is the community at large that benefits? Or should R and D be paid for by the carrier?

It is a profitless task arguing about who should pay. In the long run R and D should pay for itself: that is why R and D is carried out—to save costs or increase revenue. Expenditure on R and D is not a form of charitable payment to scientists: it is business-like expenditure based on the expectation of an adequate return. If the question is, who should pay for wasteful or wasted effort in research and development, that is another matter. According to normal business principles the owners of the capital in the business that did the research would suffer the loss. The chances are that in the end, if research and development does cost something, that cost is passed on from manufacturer to carrier and from carrier to the customer. If publicly owned transport undertakings are allowed to make losses we might then regard the community generally as bearing some of the cost of R and D.

Sometimes this question is posed in a slightly different form. Who should *initially* bear the cost of R and D, manufacturer or carrier? BOAC have complained about the burden of the cost they must bear, in bringing aircraft into service. Again it is not significant in a business setting who bears the cost initially. The whole aim of business is to cover costs by returns from customers, no matter how far back costs arise. The argument would never have arisen had BOAC been a profitable airline.

It is, however, very relevant for the transport industry to ask *at what point* research and development should be conducted. Certain fundamental investigation will be going on all the time. The fundamental dynamics of the motion of a vehicle on a track, and the fundamental aerodynamics of a vehicle moving through the air are the sorts of fields in which we would expect there to be constant research. Some research must be conducted long before plans are made for manufacturing, as these plans depend so much on the result of research. Other research is best done at the prototype production stage. At this stage a company can often begin a programme of development, which can continue through the period of manufacture of production models. Some research and development is appropriate to the stage of initial trials of production models: some will have to be delayed until equipment has been put into service on a transport system. Choosing the right point at which to do particular pieces of research and development is often a matter of close liaison between manufacturer and carrier.

There are some important differences between doing research and development in the transport industry, and doing it in many other industries. The circumstances of the laboratory are not so far removed from those of a modern, smoothly-run factory. The gap has been narrowed by companies making their factories more like laboratories. But on-the-line conditions in a transport undertaking are not conducive to the experimental methods of the laboratory. In doing research in a manufacturing industry the conditions of the factory can be reproduced in the laboratory; and in doing development the conditions of the laboratory can be reproduced on the factory floor. This is not easy in transport. It is not easy to bring all the 'open-air' variables of transport into the laboratory in full confidence that none has been omitted. It is even more difficult to bring all the variations in human conduct into the laboratory. It is usually essential to do a considerable amount of development in the light of operational experience. An interesting illustration of this point occurred in airlines that found that their aircraft cabin floors would not stand up to the weight of women brought to bear on the area of a stiletto heel. The scientist working on transport problems does not just have to discover the interaction of one piece of equipment with another piece of equipment in controlled atmospheric conditions. He has also to discover the interaction of equipment and human beings in uncontrollable atmospheric and behavioural conditions.

In the transport industry R and D must involve a great deal of study of the behaviour of operatives, equipment and customers under actual operating conditions. This may cause a tendency for more R and D to be conducted within individual undertakings rather than by specialist research organisations.

Part III

The Individual Manager

CHAPTER XIX

THE INDIVIDUAL MANAGER IN A TRANSPORT BUSINESS

In this book a case has been made for regarding transport as a special sort of business. In external relations passengers are unusual customers; the State has an unusually large say in the industry; the general public has an unusual interest in it; and so on. In internal relations, organisations generally reflect the special position of passengers, for example, *vis-à-vis* the production process. The raw materials of organisation are at one point passengers and their belongings, and at other points vehicles, track and terminals. This makes for unusual distinctions between what is technical and what is not. Organisation reflects the dangers and the need for strong discipline. Industrial relations are affected by the extent to which the economic life of a community depends on transport, and managements' bargaining powers are affected by the perishability of the product. In the various forms of special management, and their relationship with general management, there are innumerable instances of transport peculiarities, ranging from difficulties in raising equity capital, to difficulties in fully developing equipment before it goes into service.

It is important that managers in transport should study these peculiarities, because without an understanding of them, they have only normal business concepts to guide them in their task of managing. And normal business concepts will not guide them through all their difficulties.

Having said this, and having established the implications of the particular nature of transport, we must face the dangers of treating transport undertakings as if they were not businesses. Despite all the distinctions, to manage a transport undertaking successfully it is necessary to treat it, by and large, like any other business. Any other path leads to financial tangles and eventual distortion of the economic life of the community. Much damage has already been done in Britain, and elsewhere, by transport managers not behaving like business managers, but behaving at worst like amateur transport enthusiasts, and at best like public benefactors. The latter role is often spoilt by expecting a grateful public to take all that is offered at any price.

An exaggerated sense of public duty may be born of a real need for managers in the middle ranks to have faith in what they are doing. Those at the top are usually preoccupied with problems of balancing the books. The average operative does not need to believe in his work: he is busy making ends meet. But middle managers, with minds neither oppressed by the finalities of business economy, nor by the trifles of domestic economy, look for a belief in the worthwhileness of their job. This is accompanied by a worry that the alternative is a 'couldn't-care-less' attitude, manifestly dangerous in the transport industry. Many managers in transport undertakings feel they have not discovered the right attitude to their work. The trouble is that in seeking to avoid the extreme of carelessness they may fall into extremes of 'worthwhileness'.

Transport managers are basically in an enviable position. Their product is not as trivial as those of many other businesses, whose managers have to convince themselves of the value of what they are doing. Transport can, and often does, serve the most serious ends. Some of them clearly involve issues of life and death. On the other hand, not all journeys are necessary. Some travel is frivolous. But although transport is not always essential, it is reasonable to regard it as generally helpful. This is a mental luxury, denied to so many managers, that should not be over-indulged by magnifying the benefits of travel.

It is easier for managers in the production functions of passenger and freight, vehicle and maintenance control, to feel the worthwhileness of their job. It is not so easy for managers specialising in, say, finance, purchasing and research and development. They do not constantly experience reactions of customers to product, and to process of production. Their mental comfort may well call for providing some contact with customers.

From the idea that providing transport is a worthwhile job, it is easy to move on to the idea that transport must be provided at any cost. The idea is usually epitomised by phrases like 'business versus public utility' and 'profit versus social service'. The thought is superficially attractive: why should so obviously beneficial a thing like transport be effected by rather 'shady' commercial considerations like profit? And so we get transport managers torn between desires to behave like businessmen and to behave like public benefactors.

These split-levels in the human mind are at best uncomfortable, and at worst destructive of happiness and effective living and working. In this case the risks involved are unnecessary. The dichotomy is self-made. There is no real conflict between 'profit' and 'public service'. They are not competing ends: the former is not an end at all; it is simply a measure of the latter, true end. Profit is a measure of whether the public service is worth the price charged for it. There are undeniably other measures. There are, for example, the considered opinions of governments, consumer councils, local trade associations, and last but not least the opinion of the management of the undertakings providing the public service. But profit as a measure has one great advantage over all these opinions. It takes into account both the *cost* of providing the service, and the views of the customers regarding the *price* of the service. Opinions generally fail to take into account one or other of these factors.

The profit measure is necessary in transport undertakings to give managers a sense of perspective, to give them more guidance in their day-to-day conduct of business. Some costly mistakes have been made in our national undertakings, in the name of public service, prestige and even the flag. Perhaps all managers should have experience of some other business before they come to transport.

The individual manager loses 'tone' without an easily understood goal that is common to all his fellows. There are no spiritual substitutes for the age-old earthy measures of business success.

Next to the sands of idealism are the rocks of legend. The popular image of the captains of the industry is rooted in tales of a time when travel was an adventure, particularly at sea. A vessel was something beset by forces without logic or design, tossed by chance and dependent upon some mysterious fate. This demanded fatalistic attitudes from the merchant venturers who entrusted their fortunes to a voyage, and from the men in command. The sea-captain was a man for whom special prayers were said, because of the dangerous nature of his calling, and because at times only God could help him.

The weather-beaten, tough old salt, who had lived through harrowing experiences, was recognisable. The value of his experience lay chiefly in his ability to live through even more harrowing experiences. His resigned acceptance of all that the elements could throw at him was necessary in an age when men could do so little to help him. But this fatalistic attitude is not the right approach for an up-to-date transport man. Scientists and geographers have discovered a lot about the behaviour of the atmosphere, and about the composition of the surface of the earth. The area of the unknown has been much reduced. Scientists and engineers have produced equipment to stand up to known stresses and strains of its environment. A grin-and-bear-it attitude is not the right one to produce new fog-warning systems, weather radar, heated windscreens and blind-landing systems. There is not much room left for the old-salt mentality among transport managers. In a sense the new transport manager has to be a bit of an old woman, unwilling to put up with minor trials and tribulations. Problems are there to be solved, not to be put up with.

The next legend to dispose of is that transport men are men of action and not men of speech, on the grounds that only action can save the day when the boiler bursts, the brakes fail, the steering goes, and so on. But transport managers can no longer rely upon personal prowess as men of action. They must be thinkers who look for trouble, and do not wait for it. They must be blamed for failing to foresee it, not for failing to cope with it. Their plans must be to prevent, or minimise consequence of material failure and human error. Their plans must include the paradox of quiet 'routine' drills for situations of emergency.

Finally, we have the image of the bluff and hearty hail-fellow-well-met type of transport man, bursting with goodwill towards all customers. He is rightly determined that the customers' interests will be put first. Again, he is a product of bygone days; days when customers needed reassuring; and needed the confidence inspired by a warm-hearted human being at the helm. Today the customers' confidence is won mainly in office, drawing offices and workshops.

Leaving these legendary figures, we come to two contemporary extremists. The first are the men with a deep-seated belief in process of production. They believe that all the ills of business are curable by changes in production habits. This manifests itself in a tendency to plough more and more money into perfecting production long after diminishing returns have made the effort unprofitable. Then there is the natural satisfaction to be obtained from a transport system in good working order. There is the fascination of process, or system. The smallest subtraction does not seem to merely reduce the size; it threatens the existence of system. The 'system' or 'route pattern' takes on a life of its own, divorced from the public it serves. The system becomes worth believing in for its own sake. If, in the end, customers make it clear that they do not like the system, at the prices charged for it, then it is easy to believe that the customers are misguided. The next step is to convert customers to management's thinking by way of subsidy.

The second contemporary extremism is that of the professional man. In this case the engineer, or the doctor, or the accountant, or the teacher in industry aims at a professional perfection, despite the damage it may do to the business. Business is essentially a balancing of a number of efforts, at a level below the maximum of each, because of the scarcity of resources. This reconciliation of optima is achieved among the primary functions of finance, purchasing, production, marketing, personnel, research and development, by the authoritative relationships among general and special management. The advocacy of special managers is resolved into the best interests of the business by the judgement of general managers. There is no court of appeal beyond the general management of the business. General management and no other represent the best business interests of the undertaking.

But it is not unknown for a manager contributing secondary, professional functions to clash with general management, to an extent that threatens the authority-framework of a business. This the professional man achieves by referring to an overriding authority that is outside the business. It may be to a code of conduct laid down by a professional association like the BMA or to an academic discipline like that of the scientist. Whichever it is, it is bad for business. If a professional man feels he cannot compromise his professional standards even within the authoritative framework of business, he ought to stay outside of business and provide his service on a contractual basis. If he agrees to go into a business organisation, he should be prepared to give that organisation his loyalty.

Lastly, it must be said that the future of the transport industry lies with men with highly trained minds, grounded in academic disciplines, and tuned to business values. Men with minds like those of Lord Douglas of Kirtleside and Dr Beeching will always be needed at the top of Britain's transport undertakings, in order to give them crisp, businesslike leadership.

INDEX